THE SCRIPT

THE SCRIPT

THE 100% ABSOLUTELY PREDICTABLE
THINGS MEN DO WHEN THEY CHEAT

ELIZABETH LANDERS and **VICKY MAINZER**

New York

Library of Congress Cataloging-in-Publication Data

ISBN 1-4013-0228-9

Hyperion books are available for special promotions and premiums. For details contact Michael Rentas, Assistant Director, Inventory Operations, Hyperion, 77 West 66th Street, 11th Floor, New York, New York 10023, or call 212-456-0133.

FIRST EDITION

10 9 8 7 6 5 4 3 2 1

ACKNOWLEDGMENTS

The authors express their deep appreciation to Dr. Thomas Blume; Leslie Keenan; Kevin Kalb and Frank Zuber of Stone House Digital Inc.; Renee Chernus; Jane Landers; Alisa J. Kim, Book Passage; Mary Ann Sears; Mildred Kluger; Val Rantz; Kay Stewart; Joanie Silverstein; Barbara Kramer; Jason Baruch and Neil Rosini of Franklin, Weinrib, Rudell & Vassallo, New York; Marin Suites Hotel; State Farm agents Jon Lam and Ed Lazar; and Enterprise Rent-A-Car at the San Francisco Airport.

Thank you to the many people who made the writing of this book possible, including, first and foremost, Wendy Sherman and Kelly Notaras.

CONTENTS

THE SCRIPT

INTRODUCTION

It seems ludicrous that men who cheat follow a script, but they do. It's the same words and actions every time. Among rich and poor, big city and small town, in most all ethnic groups, among the young, old, and middle-aged, with men from all kinds of backgrounds. And the thing is, it's EXACTLY the same story. Almost always in the same order. As if there were a script.

It's funny, it's sad, and it's utterly amazing—men do and say exactly the same things in exactly the same order when they are unfaithful. We think cheating revolves around love and sex and intrigue and illicit encounters—and it does. But men also talk and act as if there were a script.

All of us have probably heard bits and pieces from the Script. We know about the secrecy, the lying, the unusual phone calls, the lipstick on the shirt collar—and we all probably know some of the ways the Script has changed with the advent of cell phones, the Internet, and credit cards.

This is the first book to expose the cheating man's script and the total predictability of most everything he says or does. It lays out the entire Script, act by act, scene by scene, and line by line, so every woman knows how the performance unfolds.

We have found that men talk and act as if there were a manual. And they all have a copy. And they took the same course where this was the textbook. And one and the same teacher taught this course wherever it was given. And these cheating men attended every session. And they remembered everything they learned. And they remembered the order in which to do it.

And the Script was written nowhere until now.

We discovered the Script in conversation. Friends since our children were in high school together in San Francisco, we stayed in touch after both of us went through divorce, and Vicky moved away. As we talked about our work, the organizations we were involved in, and the odds and ends of life, we realized that in one area we were hearing the same story over and over. Unfaithful men all acted alike. Just like they were following a script. This was confirmed through conversations and correspondence with hundreds of people throughout the country. The identical play was being reenacted unfaithful man after unfaithful man. We began to collect these stories and realized there was something more here.

We knew we were onto something from the number of stories we heard, and the level of interest we found from everyone we mentioned this idea to. This issue affects women from all walks of life, all socioeconomic groups, all ages, all backgrounds, all parts of the country. Every woman who experiences an unfaithful husband feels confused and baffled by his contradictory statements and behavior. She starts to believe that she really must be crazy, unappealing, selfish, and unloving, just as her husband says. This book helps women to understand that it is all part of the Script.

Intense shame, embarrassment, and taboos often keep a woman from confiding in close friends and relatives when confronted with her husband's infidelity. This book is a way to compare notes without having to broach this difficult topic with others. It's a way to learn. Many women wonder, "Is it just me, or does every woman feel this way?" Every woman feels this way.

The book is based on real-life stories, but all names and details are fictional. We've talked to hundreds of women and men, and to experts in the field: lawyers, therapists, doctors, financial advisers, and psychologists.

We know for many readers the questions will be: Is *my* husband cheating? How do I know? What should I do? Throughout the book we include both Tips—suggestions on what actions and attitudes we think will be most helpful for you—and Boxes—the boxes are specifically intended to show you how you can interrupt the Script.

We don't believe all men are unfaithful. We don't believe all men who follow the first part of the Script cheat. We do believe there are steps you can take and things you can do to protect yourself in the event they do. We also believe there are things you can do, once you are aware of the Script, that can help you in your marriage. Most of all, though, we want you to know you are not alone; to know that the way it happened to you is the way it always happens; to laugh at the absurdity of it all; and to arm yourself for what is going to happen next—to be ahead of the game because you know the Script.

OVERTURE

OVERTURE

Only the percussionist is present in the orchestra pit below the stage and the drum roll is barely audible, nearly drowned out by the sounds of everyday life outside the theater. It's so low that you pay no attention. You don't even hear the loud, rapid roll that usually comes at the end, presaging something important to come. You're paying more attention to the sound of a violin and a flute, and a very mellifluous and soothing tenor rising above.

This tenor is singing: "I Would Never Do That."

SCENE 1: "I WOULD NEVER DO THAT"

Sharon and Nick are leaving Nick's company's office reception when Sharon asks her husband, "Where did Jackie get that diamond bracelet? She couldn't possibly buy such an expensive piece of jewelry on her secretary's salary. She told me it came from Tiffany's, but of course I couldn't ask her how she got it."

Nick answers, "Oh, I know how she got it. Don, the senior VP you met a few months ago, gave it to her. They're having an affair."

Sharon thinks for a second and then says, "But Don's married, isn't he? Didn't I meet his wife, Joan? How do you know they're having an affair?"

"I could just tell," Nick says.

"My gosh. What goes on!" Sharon exclaims.

"Yeah, it's not a good scene all around. I tell you, I would never do that to you."

We have found that almost every woman who finds out that she has an unfaithful husband remembers her husband saying several years before, "I Would Never Do That," while commenting disapprovingly on a man who has just been unfaithful.

This line in the Script gives you no sense that anything might be amiss. Only in hindsight (unless you've read this book and can be alert to it as it's happening) will you see that this was the moment he began sending signals that he was alert to other possibilities, to other ways to act out his life.

At the time, your reaction is the opposite of suspicion. You are grateful and reassured that your husband is so completely different. You think, "He really understands how wrong it is to cheat. How wonderful to be married to someone who can see how immoral this is. I am really proud to be married to a man who is so upstanding."

You feel sympathy for Don's wife and a little glee at hearing the latest gossip. Then you put the whole story out of your mind—it's just another story of someone else's misfortune.

Nancy and Jim are straightening up after dinner when Nancy says to Jim, "Say, how's Paul? I was thinking of him today when someone mentioned artists who then go on to tech jobs. You haven't mentioned him in a while."

"Oh, Paul," Jim responds. "I guess he thinks he's a bohemian again. He just left Kathy and the kids and moved in with his secretary. She must be twenty years younger than he is."

"What?" Nancy stares at him. "Kathy's so sweet and they have the greatest kids. They've been married a long time. His secretary? How could he do that?"

Jim shakes his head. "No, it's not right and it's making things very awkward in the office. I would never do that."

You feel lucky to have a husband who is so much better than other men, a husband who is completely faithful and caring, who lives by what he believes in. You think, "That could never happen to me with a man as virtuous and devoted as my husband. I can put that worry totally out of my mind, thank goodness."

This is a very natural reaction on your part, and it may be just the one he wants you to have. He is thinking that what Paul has done sounds appealing. But if he criticizes Paul, the last thing that would occur to you, now or in the future, is that your own husband might be open to cheating. By assuring you he would never do that, he has thrown you off his track.

SCENE 2: "YOU NEED TO SEE A PSYCHIATRIST"

Maggie is sitting at the kitchen table going over the checkbook, and staring at the remodeling books the contractor has just brought over. Joe comes in from outside, looks at her, and says, "You're depressed. You need to see a psychiatrist."

"Need to see a psychiatrist? What do you mean?"

"I mean you need to see a psychiatrist. Look at you sitting hunched over all that paper, fixated on all those picture books. You can't seem to make any decisions. That's depressed."

"I don't feel depressed. I'm just trying to get some of this paper-work done and figure out what to do with the kitchen."

"Have it your way then, but I'm telling you, you need help."

Maggie feels insulted and confused. "Why would anyone think balancing the checkbook and looking at remodeling ideas is act-ing depressed? Did he read about depressed women somewhere? Did someone else tell him I seem depressed? He seems so defi-nite about it and so critical. He's sort of saying that if I don't re-alize it and don't seek help then I'm even worse off than I realize. He's telling me I don't want to be the best I can be, and he won't love me anymore if I don't try to be the best I can be. Maybe I *should* go see a psychiatrist. But then again I don't feel de-pressed."

He's building a case, though not consciously. It's the same case he'll use later—even though he doesn't even know there will be a later. It may be years before he presents the final summation.

He's following the Script. He's heard men play out all these scenes many times, and he has learned this is a good way to begin. Cast-ing you as the sick, depressed, and troubled one gets the audience in the right mood to understand and applaud the rest of the play, especially his character: the good guy. He's beginning to set up the contrasts between you and him. Later, when the news breaks, the stage will be set so that people who would ordinarily cast him as the villain will do just the opposite. They'll say, "He's done his best to get along with a crazy, depressed woman and has given her every chance to get help. But she refused to get better." He's the good guy. You're the problem.

Watch this man act.

The "Director"

The "director" sums up the essence of the Script. He is the little voice in every man's head. The director passes the story down from generation to generation, always adapting it to the mores of the times.

Carl and Bill are walking out to the parking lot after a long day's work.

"She's crazy, out of control. The doctor even says so. When I was in for my checkup I was telling him that if I just want to spend a couple of nights out with the guys she's all up in arms, asking me why I'm not home more. She wants me home all the time. She's always wanting me to go places with the kids. She's out of control."

Carl just listens as Bill lets loose with all his problems at home.

"I thought all along she was unbalanced. I knew Dr. Feller would agree with me. Sure enough, he says she needs help."

Before our man starts his speaking part he has to get into the right frame of mind. The Script has even taught him the thoughts that will accomplish this. He's thinking to himself, "I'm a good person. I'm doing all the right things to make her happy. She's still not happy. Therefore there's something really wrong with her." The director has told him to keep playing these thoughts over and over in his head so that later on his spoken lines will carry real feeling.

If he were reciting his real feelings aloud now and listening to what he was saying, that would mean recognizing he has some problems and that he might have to ask for help in addressing them. Not easy for our man. Many men find this difficult, so they make you the problem.

He has also started talking to others because he cares about the court of world opinion. You're upside-down crazy, and he's upright. Whatever he does in the future, he has already colored you in a very convenient light.

The Wagners and their neighbors are having a last cup of coffee after their annual Labor Day picnic, when Flo Wagner says, "Did you know that the Goldens are having problems? I heard they just can't get along. What do you think it is?"

"I'll tell you what it is. He should send her to see a psychiatrist," her neighbor Rick says.

Flo hears this and thinks to herself that maybe Nancy Golden *is* a little erratic. Maybe Rick is right and Nancy's husband should get her to a shrink.

Men have learned the Script so well that a man who doesn't even *know* the couple immediately suggests that the husband should send his wife to a shrink. Other women can be pulled along too, becoming convinced that the wife is the source of the problem because she is unbalanced.

Gaslight

This is the most extreme example we've ever heard of to make the wife think she's crazy. It's just like the movie with Ingrid Bergman.

Teresa pulls up to the gas pump, takes out her wallet, and reaches for her credit card. But the spot where she always keeps it is empty. The card is not there. She thinks to herself, "Where is it? What happened to it?

Could I have left it at the grocery yesterday? I'll just pay
cash and figure out what I did with the card when I get
home."

That evening, Teresa mentions to her husband, Hal, that she
can't find her credit card. Hal tells her she's careless, totally
disorganized, and really has to pull herself together. He
says, "Call the bank, get another card, and please don't lose
it again."

When Teresa takes out her wallet at the florist a couple of
weeks later she is horrifed to discover again that she can't
find her credit card. She is forced to leave without the flowers and feels embarrassed and foolish for having lost her
card a second time. That night she tells Hal what happened
and he says, "Teresa, what's the matter with you? You can't
seem to do anything right."

When Teresa finds her card missing a third time she thinks
she must be losing her mind. Exactly what Hal intended.

Hal had been going into Teresa's purse and taking the card
with the intention of making her think she was falling apart.
She found out what Hal was doing when she happened to
walk in just as Hal was about to go into her purse the next
time.

However he sets it up to tell you you're depressed, crazy, out
of control, or falling to pieces, the goal is the same: he's trying to make *you* the problem.

The Charge: guilty by reason of insanity

TIP: DON'T PLEAD GUILTY

Expose the false charges by asking for the evidence.

Don't let the "guilty by reason of insanity" charge go unanswered. Ask him exactly what it is that you are doing that he thinks requires you to see a psychiatrist. He may say that you are depressed, crazy, or that you act unbalanced. Or he may try to change the topic. Ask him again what specific symptoms of craziness or depression he sees.

To avoid having to come up with evidence that doesn't exist, he may tell you that he was just joking when he said you need to see a shrink, or that you take things too seriously and you shouldn't worry about it.

Or he may answer that you're obviously depressed and troubled because you're always tired and have no energy. If you answer that it's no wonder you're always tired given you have to juggle the laundry, the children, the bills, the shopping, the cleaning, and possibly a full- or part-time job, he'll likely respond that that just proves how out of touch with real life you are. Instead, try asking him if he can help you with some of the things on your plate.

If you don't get satisfactory answers, find a therapist who can help you with your relationship. Whatever you do, don't let the charges go unanswered.

TIP: GO FOR COUNSELING

Try your best to get him to go with you for counseling. In particular, try to go together for the first appointment. If you've gone alone he may have the feeling when he comes with you the next time that he's already been branded as the bad guy.

Let's say your husband refuses to go but you *do* make an appointment with a therapist. When you walk into the therapist's office and are greeted warmly and sympathetically, you will likely feel better immediately. It seems like the charges will be dropped.

But it may be that you're about to be: Charged Again By Reason of Expert Testimony.

TIP: DON'T PLEAD GUILTY

If you sit down in a therapist's office and hear "Dear, I'm sorry you're suffering from this disorder. I'm going to treat you," don't plead guilty. Do not accept a judgment from a professional that says you're impaired.

You may come into the therapist's office saying, "My husband says I'm depressed." It's easy for the therapist to simply accept your husband's "diagnosis" and proceed to treat you on this basis. In truth you may or may not be depressed. There are probably many other things to look at.

Find another therapist who doesn't assume you're defective.

TIP: IF YOU'RE A SMALL-TOWN GIRL

If you live in a smaller town, finding a therapist (and possibly finding *another* therapist) may be totally impractical suggestions. Availability, distance, and financial considerations may be roadblocks. Also, in a small town, it may be difficult to visit a counselor quietly, as you would probably prefer at this time. The last thing you need is to have the whole town buzzing about why you were seen walking into a shrink's office.

Here are some ideas for help no matter where you live:

The clergy. Best of all are pastors who have been trained in marriage and family counseling. The regional office of your religious denomination can provide a list of pastors with this training.

Social workers, nurse practitioners, and psychiatric nurses. Again, best of all are those specially trained in marriage and family counseling. Your state licensing board for each profession can provide a list of those closest to you or who can give telephone help.

Couples support programs, marriage enrichment groups, or self-help groups for couples. Most likely you will find a program like this through a church, synagogue, or other religious institution. They may operate with or without a leader.

The Internet. There are several sites on the Internet. One that's helpful is www.therapistlocator.net.

If the above resources still present difficulties or are not appealing to you, consider talking to a relative you feel you can trust.

TIP: START TALKING TO YOURSELF.
KEEP A JOURNAL.

If you don't have the time, money, or access to a therapist, the next best thing is keeping a journal. It is valuable even if you are seeing a therapist.

Writing your thoughts down forces you to examine them. As you're thinking "Who's crazy here?" it will give you a better understanding of what's going on. Keeping a record of the facts as they occur may also be useful in challenging his version of events later.

An Early Warning

The good news is he's giving you an early warning. While the signal is weak, misdirected, and insulting, when he says to you, "You need to see a psychiatrist," you know he has started on the Script. You shouldn't let it go as an idle comment, joke, or meaningless remark. Be on your guard: he may now proceed to other lines of the Script.

SCENE 3: "I KEEP TELLING YOU TO . . ."

The kids have scattered from the dinner table to the computer, homework, and the telephone as Tracy loads the dishwasher. Her husband, Scott, hands her some dishes, then comes over to stand next to her and says, "Tracy, I'm thinking you'd be happier if you were going to school. Why don't you take a course at State and get started on your teaching degree the way you've always wanted to? It would give you some outside interests and you could get a job here in Chevy Chase after you finish."

"I don't know. With the four kids and all the things they're doing and now you're out of town more with your new job, I don't know where I'd squeeze it in," Tracy says.

"Well, think about it," Scott says.

Sarah and Hank are getting ready for a cocktail party when Sarah takes off the dress she has just put on and throws it on the bed. "Guess I gained some weight since I bought this. It doesn't look that good. I'm going to wear the same dress I wore last week."

"You have an awful lot of too-tight dresses sitting in the closet. Buy a gym membership, then you'll be at the weight you want to be. I've offered it to you."

"I don't know when I would go. Who's going to watch Timmy and the baby?"

"Well, I've offered it to you."

"Oh gosh, the day just seems to go by and I don't get anything done," Jen says to her husband as she's still doing laundry at ten o'clock at night.

"I keep telling you to get up an hour earlier and do all these things in the morning. Then your evenings would be free and we could spend time together," her husband, Josh, says.

"Getting up an hour earlier won't put much of a dent in what I have to do. And I need that extra hour's sleep," Jen says.

"I'm telling you it will give you a more organized day. And I keep telling you you'll sleep better if you don't go to bed so exhausted. You haven't been sleeping well."

Mindy is sitting in her office finishing up the last problem for the day with her boss, Joe, when the phone rings.

"Mindy, it's me. What're you doing? Shouldn't you have finished up already? Who's in your office with you?"

"Oh, Charlie," Mindy says to her husband, who has called her multiple times that day as he does almost every day, "it's just this last thing we have to finish."

"Well, what is it? I can probably help you solve the problem," Charlie says.

"Thanks, but we can work it out. I'll be home in an hour or so."

"I keep telling you to let me help you out, but you don't listen. Fine, you work it out on your own," Charlie says.

Psychiatrist, teacher, personal trainer. What can't he do?

But is he doing it to be caring or controlling? You may think that calling you eight or ten times a day is a sign of love and genuine interest. But he may be doing it to try to control everything you do. When he tells you to get up earlier so you have more time in the evening to spend together with him, it may be because he genuinely loves you and he enjoys spending more time with you, or it may be because he wants all your time and attention to be focused on him.

If he's controlling, it means he wants things to go his way, and it could be an indication that he is self-centered. It could mean he is the opposite of caring, and it could mean he would be willing to be unfaithful.

When he says "I keep telling you to . . ." or "why don't you . . ." or "I've offered it to you . . ." or "if only you would . . ." or "I'm only trying to help . . ." and you're trying to figure out whether it's caring or controlling, then the answer is in your gut.

TIP: THE ANSWER IS IN THE AIR— AND IN YOUR GUT.

The answer is in the air, in the words hanging unsaid. But they're seeping into your gut and you feel them. If the words you feel hanging in the air after he says I Keep Telling You To . . . are:

I Keep Telling You To . . . *and if you don't do it you're not very smart* or

. . . *and if you don't do it you don't know how to take advice* or

. . . *and if you don't do it you can't see that I'm right* or

. . . *and if you don't do it you can't see that you need improvement* or

. . . *and if you don't do it I won't love you anymore . . .*

then his intention might be more controlling than caring.

If he Keeps Telling You To . . . over and over, and his tone of voice is not entirely caring, and you've heard him play out other parts of the Script, and it comes with a disquieting feeling in your gut—then it might not be caring.

If you have to ask yourself if it's caring or controlling, this is a strong sign the answer is "controlling."

However, if your gut tells you his words do carry a caring feeling, be glad he does care and say thank you to him. There will always be un-asked-for advice and suggestions in a marriage. If you get that loving feeling from his interest, then trust it.

Pushed and Pulled

You will feel buffeted by two air currents pushing you in opposite directions. One current pushing you is the disquieting feeling telling you to look at what's happening. The other current is the sense of foreboding pushing you away from looking because you are afraid of what you will find.

As fearful as you are, better to look now. If you choose to ignore it, it may come back to hit you in the face.

BEFORE HE LEAVES

The curtain goes up for the first act and the stage is full of activity. As your eye sweeps across it, you see a panorama of everyday life. Nothing remarkable. A family at home in the evening, people talking in a carpool van, three men working together to help a neighbor plant a tree. You wonder why you came to see this play. You heard it was spectacular but you think, "This is not interesting. This is what I see every day." It's not even clear who the male lead is, the starring actor you thought you were going to see. You think, "I'm not hearing anything I didn't know before."

You will! The Script is under way, even if there are no words yet to be heard, not even in his own head. He is feeling things he is not consciously aware of. All you hear is noisy silence. The noise of everyday, ordinary life. Silent signals emanating from him.

What he is feeling is a vague unhappiness, a dissatisfaction, a lack of recognition. After he has worked so hard at his job to provide for his wife and children, he feels like nobody cares about *his* needs.

SCENE 1: "WHAT ABOUT ME?"

It's ten o'clock on Saturday night and Kirk is fooling with his computer and thinking to himself, "Man, was this a hard week. I was the one who raced over to Downer's Grove because Sam was out playing golf with his supposed clients. Had to meet that deadline or we wouldn't even have been one of the bidders. We got it done because I covered for everyone who wasn't there, who didn't have their stuff done on time, and who wrote incompetent proposals. And did anyone at the office say 'Good job?' No. But they never do. Yeah, the kids were mad because I missed their games Wednesday night. Don't they know I'm doing this for them? I hope Sally realizes all I do for her. I'm not sure she does."

Sally pokes her head into the den and says, "Kirk, I know you love fiddling on your computer and you're tired but we've got to pack the car for tomorrow or we won't get away on time for Todd's class picnic in Woodpines. It'll just take a little bit."

Kirk says, "Okay, okay," but he's thinking, "Have to miss going sailing again tomorrow. When am I going to have some time for *my* fun? *What about me?*"

Ben and Greg have finished lunch in the cavernous MegaCon cafeteria and are shooting the breeze until it's time to hit their desks again.

"I've gotta leave on time today," Greg says, "because Deanna told me she'll be at her office until late."

"Oh, so she got that job?" Ben asks.

"Yeah, she got the job," Greg answers. "They told her she's wonderful. But I'm telling you if you walked into our house it doesn't look so wonderful."

"I know what you mean," Ben says. "I work, work, work all day and what do I get when I get home? It's frozen pizza and a messy house." Ben thinks, "What about me?"

"Same thing in my house," Greg says, also thinking, "What about me?"

You're listening to the play but you keep wondering why anyone would bother to put this on stage. It's just like everyday life. The male lead is speaking the lines a million men have spoken before.

It's his feelings that make up the Script now but these feelings of unhappiness and lack of recognition are not always explicit in the spoken lines. Nor are they even explicit in his head. But the essence of his feelings is that he gives, gives, gives, works, works, works, and nobody says thank you or shows any appreciation for what he has given. What's more, in his mind, it seems everybody's always asking him to do more, more, more but again giving nary a thought to his needs.

But soon, in the ordinary course of everyday life, he happens upon a totally different feeling.

Be Exciting, Supportive, Understanding, and Appreciative

What *don't* you have to do?

Yes, it's true. It often feels like it's *you* who has to shoulder the major responsibility for the emotional part of your marriage, in addition to everything else you have to do and maybe in the face of a dismissive, critical, or superior attitude from him. Emotional upkeep should be his responsibility as well, but he may not know how to discuss his feelings.

It's up to you to bring up topics that involve feelings; sex is especially important to talk about. It may not be easy because his reaction may be dismissive or critical. But push on. You may strike gold and he may react with feeling, interest, appreciation, and the desire to talk.

SCENE 2: "WOW, THAT FELT GOOD"

In his head vague and unidentified feelings of unhappiness and discontent are swirling when he comes upon the Momentary Encounter. In a few brief moments he feels something quite different, something good. He feels happy.

Will is teaching three different economics courses this semester at Bedford University, two big sections and one seminar. It's a lot of work but he has some excellent students who make it all worthwhile. Just yesterday, Andrea came up to him and thanked him for helping her to understand that complicated statistical formula. She showed him the beginning of her final paper and he made some suggestions. She was so appreciative. She smiled a "thank you" at him and Will walked back to the faculty office building on top of the world. He had never realized how attractive Andrea was. He thought to himself, "Wow, that felt good."

It was very brief, almost insignificant, but it gave Will a high.

It's been so long since he felt that way—maybe not since the early days of courting his wife.

It's been very quiet today in the Beautiful Home Carpet Showroom. The salesmen are mostly standing around talking to each other. The only call for Clay has been his wife telling him to please pick up some gas for the power mower so he can mow the lawn when he gets home. Clay is straightening the Oriental rug section when a woman comes in and walks right over to the two-foot pile of Azhaks he has just rearranged.

"Ooh, I want to see the ones at the bottom," she says.

"Certainly, ma'am." Clay's athletic physique is mightily exhibited as he pulls back twelve heavy rugs, stopping at the blue one he has found appeals to women.

"Wouldn't this be beautiful in your home?" Clay asks. "Oh, my name is Clay. Here's my card."

"I'm Julie. I could never whip those rugs back like that. How did you know I'd love the blue one?" Julie sits down on the rug to feel the pile and looks up at Clay. "Yeah, Clay, I love it. Could you bring it to my house so I could try it out?"

"Sure could."

Clay thinks "Julie certainly is good-looking and she loves what I showed her. Wow, that felt good."

It was just a minute or two, but in that brief time Clay felt really happy. So much better than his general feelings of discontent.

Ryan is tired after walking around with a crying three-month-old for two hours so he's happy when Mommy takes over. He says to his wife, Alexa, "I'm going to take a break," and goes to the basement to relax a little online. Just yesterday he had seen an online ad about reconnecting with high school classmates and he thought he'd like to try to find out whatever happened to Olivia. It was thirteen years ago when they graduated, and he hasn't seen her since. He enters her name, waits, but gets no response.

Every evening he goes online hoping that he will see an answer. Nothing for a week. Then one evening he sees an e-mail he can't wait to open—"Hi Ryan. It's Olivia." With this they start to get reacquainted online.

They e-mail each other several times a day. Ryan finds that Olivia is so understanding. She sympathizes with his being stuck at home so much with the baby, who requires so much attention. She thinks his plans to buy a PizzaParty franchise and get out of his dull job are fantastic. All Alexa does is complain about how much he will be away from home if he owns a seven-day-a-week business. Recently, at the end of an e-mail, Olivia mentions how she undresses down to nothing when she comes home from work. Wow, that felt good.

Ryan feels he must try to rendezvous with Olivia. He's thrilled to find out she lives just fifty miles away.

You have a woman's intuition. You also have a woman's counterintuition.

TIP: A WOMAN'S BEST INTUITION NOW IS COUNTERINTUITION

At this point in the Script, your intuition may be telling you he's a little distant—talking to you a bit less, confiding in you a bit less. You also may notice him noticing other women. The intuitive reaction would be to discourage him from talking about other women he finds attractive. The natural feeling would be that if you let him talk about this kind of thing, it might drive him further in the direction of someone else. But you would be wrong.

It's counterintuitive but it's true—giving him the freedom, the comfort, the opportunity, even the *encourage-*

ment to talk to you about the fact that he finds other women attractive may keep his impulses to talk rather than action. It may bring him closer to you, because he will feel he can talk to you about anything.

In a way you're the woman who knows too much about him. He may fear your judgment or rejection if he opens up to you. Because of this, every other woman in the world seems to be a safer and more comfortable person to talk to. They know less about him and thus pose less of a threat.

Use this piece of counterintelligence. Be open to his talking about the fact that he finds other women attractive. This is not meant to include derogatory or demeaning comments about you from him, or about him from you. Nor does it mean allowing him to talk about his sexual fantasies if you don't like it. What it means is allowing him to be open with you, which brings you both closer together.

SCENE 3: A WORLD FULL OF POSSIBILITIES

Wow, that felt good. It happened once, it happened twice. Looking around, he sees many other possibilities to recreate that moment when he felt so happy and relieved of his malaise.

Malaise

This malaise could be:

- A MIDLIFE CRISIS. He's reaching the point where he has to reduce his expectations. He has to deal with the reality that he may not achieve the goals he had set for himself when young.

- BEING A FATHER. He doesn't have the same freedom he had when he wasn't a dad. He's feeling restless and hemmed in.

- BOREDOM. Life has fallen into a routine that's not exciting.

Warm spring weather has come to the Creshfield U campus. It is even warm enough for Will to hold his seminar outside on the campus green. Will spreads his notes and books out under a tree and reserves an area of lawn big enough for his twelve students. While he's waiting for the two o'clock start of his class he notices the warm weather has brought out a lot of students in shorts. Those two women with the Creshfield U tennis team tops and shorts sure look attractive. And isn't that Louise, the new member of the econ faculty, walking by?

It's Mike's turn to pick up all of the eight boys on his son's swim team and get them to the meet in Plano. Getting an early start, Mike arrives at the team captain's house at 6:00 A.M. He honks and out runs fourteen-year-old Jason, toting his gym bag. Jason's house is dark so he thinks everyone else must still be asleep. Not so. The door opens and Jason's mom runs after him with his extra suit. "How does she look so together, so early?" Mike wonders.

"Morning, Mike," she says. "Thanks for getting Jason to the meet. You're a wonderful dad to get up so early and pick up eight boys."

A world full of possibilities. His mind is swirling with thoughts of these attractions. Most everywhere he turns there is another desirable woman who could give him that happy feeling he's tasted so recently. "I'm open to it. Let it happen."

Some men let it rest at that—a satisfying look at the possibilities.

Alas, other men take it further, and go on to act out the rest of the Script.

Absence Does *Not* Make the Heart Grow Fonder

It's eleven o'clock at night. Julie and Tim have been arguing for an hour over who forgot to pay the credit card bill and caused the whopping interest charge they just received. There's no resolution to the argument and Julie and Tim go to bed facing opposite ways.

Morning comes and they're barely speaking. They part for the day saying only, "See you when I get home."

Don't let distance grow between you. Absence does *not* make the heart grow fonder.

Take the first step to bridge the chasm. Say "I'm sorry for what happened last night."

This is not easy to do because it seems you're almost always the one saying "I'm sorry," even when both of you have been arguing equally fiercely and each of you feels you have right on your side.

You feel you are already behind because, looking back, you see that you are almost always the one to say "I'm sorry" first.

But if he has been experiencing "Wow, that felt good" moments—and there's no way to know if he has—you are at a disadvantage. Simply because you are his wife, every other woman by definition seems easier to talk to. Every other woman seems more admiring of him, more supportive, more exciting. You are coming out the worse by comparison. If later that day he has a "Wow, that felt good" moment, and you have made a warm, inviting, and open comment like "I'm sorry," you come out looking much better. The appeal of his chance "Wow, that felt good" encounter is diminished.

The Fairer Sex

He's thinking, "You know too much about me. You don't understand me."

You think, "Gosh, I can't win."

He's thinking, "I want someone warm and open to talk to. Keep your distance."

You think, "Gosh I can't win."

He's thinking, "Can't you look enticing and exciting like all these other women? Can't you have everything in order in the house all the time?"

You think, "Gosh, I can't win. It's not fair."

It's true. In a way you *can't* win. And it's not fair. All we can say is that there's a lot in this life that's not fair to the fairer sex.

Continuing to keep your journal here can help. It will allow you to vent all your frustrations without yelling at him, and it will also help you document his baffling behavior so you can see its contradictions.

SCENE 4: PRE-SEPARATION SEPARATING

Curtis comes home a little late one night. He didn't even eat lunch today, he's been so busy. He thought it would be nice just to sit down and have dinner with his family. The noise that greets him as he walks in from the garage is deafening. The kids are fighting over some game. The family room and dinner table offer no signs of a peaceful dinner, or any dinner.

Curtis calls out, "Hey, anyone care that I'm home?" Little Tommy says, "Hi, Dad," and goes back to fighting with his sister. No sign of Mary. Curtis throws his jacket down and looks into the kitchen. Mary is on the phone intently talking to what sounds like one of her yoga class friends. He walks up to her and says, "Any chance of dinner here?" Mary motions him away and mouths that she'll just be another few minutes. Curtis is thinking that he might feel better going back to the office. His family doesn't even seem to care that he came home.

He's said nothing to you directly about being unhappy or wanting to leave you. He may well have done nothing that would make him an unfaithful husband. But he has experienced the "wow, that felt good" moment and, almost imperceptibly, he starts separating himself from you, your children, and your home life.

Recognizing the Script

If he's not saying anything, how can you know if he's at this stage? You will have to rely on your intuition and your knowledge of all of the Script. He may do one or two but not act out the rest. Trust your gut feeling.

Is he:

- PICKING FIGHTS?

- ACTING UNAPPRECIATED?

- NOT TALKING TO YOU?

- ACTING DISTANT?

GIL: It's already Thursday evening. I don't see that you've done a thing to prepare for Saturday night's party. We've got thirty people coming, including my boss. When do you plan to do all the cooking? Saturday at 5:00 p.m.?

KAREN: When have I ever not been ready for a party? You've said yourself that people just love the parties we give, that they're loads of fun and the food is great. I've done everything I need to do for Saturday.

GIL: You have? Where is it? What is it? All I see is a bare kitchen. And that's a miracle because it usually looks like a pigsty.

KAREN: Which is it you want? A kitchen that's a little messy because I'm getting ready for a party? Or a showplace with spic-and-span counters?

GIL: What are you talking about kitchen counters for? We're talking about the party Saturday. And I can't see that it's going to be anything like a great party. I don't know what's the matter with you. You just can't seem to get it together.

KAREN: I asked you before, when have I not given a great party? Everybody asks my advice on how to give a party. Why do you have to act like a catering inspector? Leave me alone. I've got things to do.

You're hurt that he would be so critical of something y°
well and act as cold to you as if you were the hired he
wondering how to please him. "Should I keep the kitc'
ulate," Karen asks herself, "and not make all the di<
ple love but that make such a mess? Then our part'
the raves they do. Or should I make all those <
then the kitchen is a mess. I don't know w'
happy. It seems that no matter what I do it'
him get away with all these snipes at me w'
job with parties. I have to speak up."

Just the result he intended. He intentior
you do well. You defend yourself. He '
argument, pushed you into disagr'
into acting in a way he feels he ca'
mentative, and incompetent. '
spending more time away fre

ROB:
stuf
bunc
PAULA: I
ROB: You i
mess. Pl
to pay so

live with. He also feels fully justified in spending more time looking at the World Full of Possibilities—because that brings him the happiness he deserves which he so obviously is not getting at home.

ROB: Why don't you take a weekend trip with your friends to that spa in Arizona?

PAULA: I don't know. I don't think I have the time and it would be expensive to fly there from here. And I hear the rooms there are five hundred dollars a day plus a bunch of extra charges.

ROB: Go ahead. Treat yourself. You'll enjoy going with Tina and everyone.

PAULA: But we have so many other bills to pay. I would hate to spend all that money on a spa weekend for myself.

ROB: Why not? Go. You can get all those facials and massages you love.

PAULA: I'm really not sure. What would you do? This would all be for me.

ROB: I'm telling you, don't worry. Go. I'll manage.

PAULA: Okay, I'm going. A spa weekend sounds great.

's a month later. Paula has just returned from Arizona.

When are you going to catch up on all this paperwork, all this that piled up while you were in Arizona? We've also got a of bills to pay.

ust got back. I'll get to it.

ook all that time for yourself and now we're sitting in this s the money you spent at the spa could have been used me bills.

PAULA: But, remember? You encouraged me to go.

ROB: Yeah, but not if I had to do all the cooking while you were away and now have to sit here and figure out which bills I can delay for a while.

Paula thinks to herself, "Didn't Rob push me to go on that spa weekend? I felt a little guilty from the beginning spending all that money on myself. But he kept saying, 'Go, go.' Now he's criticizing me for going."

Just the result he intended. He pushed you to do something just for yourself, maybe a little "selfish." Now he has something to criticize you for. Again, he is intentionally setting up a scene where he can paint you with a negative brush—argumentative, unpleasant, selfish, uncomprehending, dense, uncooperative.

It's as easy as painting by the numbers because he has heard the Script so many times from other men. But it leaves you puzzled and confused, because he is telling you two contradictory things and you can't get him to explain why. The next scene will give you some explanations.

TIP: INTERRUPT THE SCRIPT

Step out of the audience and be part of the play for a moment.

We will give you ideas for two completely different ways for you to play this scene.

OPTION ONE:

Don't keep asking him what's wrong. If he has, in fact, been unfaithful, he will most likely just keep telling you

that nothing is wrong. If he has just been having some fantastical thoughts, you will seem like a pest, nag, or killjoy. Back off.

Do your best to look attractive, keep your home neat, comfortable, and a place he wants to be, and show appreciation for the everyday and special things he does for you and your family. Give more attention to your husband.

Show him you are aware he is looking around by making a comment *yourself* about other women, such as, "Wow, those girls sure have cute figures." Just as the tip in Scene 2 suggested, this may stop him in his tracks.

OPTION TWO:

You sense that something is not right. You think he *may* be cheating. When you ask questions, he won't give you any answers. *Flush out the facts.*

Talk to your friends. Ask them if they feel that everything is okay with your husband. Or hire a private investigator to get the facts. If your suspicions are proven accurate, confront him. If a private investigator is not a practical choice for you, file for divorce. This may seem drastic but it will very quickly shine a light on what is really happening.

If there is no unfaithfulness, it will help you get started on seeing what the real problems are that are causing his unresponsiveness, distancing from you, and edginess.

If there is infidelity, it will also be a means to get started on solving the problems in your marriage—whether it

means working on the problems or following through with a divorce.

If You See Something, Say Something

Take a hint from the New York Underground. The New York subway system's new anti-terror campaign says, "If you see something, say something."

Add to that a bit of wisdom from pain management—"treat the pain early." Later, after it has gotten worse, it will be much more difficult—sometimes impossible—to relieve.

In other words, if you feel something is up, talk about it sooner rather than later because it will be easier to solve when it is a small problem rather than a larger one. It's true that it's not always easy to decide if something is *something* that warrants discussion with your husband or if it is truly minor and bringing it up would be making something out of nothing. See Option One. Don't *keep* bringing it up.

SCENE 5: "SHE DOESN'T UNDERSTAND ME"

Valery and Brian are looking over the shop floor as they coordinate production schedules when Valery says, "Oh my gosh, it's already two o'clock and I haven't eaten lunch yet."

Brian says, "You're right. Let's run over to Louie's and grab a bite." They walk to a small restaurant across the street and, as Brian sits down wearily in his chair, he lets out a sigh.

Valery says, "What's up for you this weekend?"

Brian says, "Oh, I don't know, a bunch of stuff. My wife has it all laid out. I'd like to go mountain biking with Harry and Glen. And that machine Glen just had installed on the shop floor, I want to think about new ways we can use it. I just need time to hang out, to think, to stretch. But Carrie doesn't understand that. She just doesn't understand me, period."

"I see. It must be hard to have all these ideas and things you want to do and no one to talk to about it," Valery says.

"Yes, I have so much to talk about, but Carrie and I have grown apart."

Marty and Nikki have been seeing each other secretly for six months and arranged yesterday to meet at 6:00 P.M. at Moonbeam, an out-of-the-way club twenty miles from Marty's home. He arrives early to secure a table way in the back. It seems Nikki must be as eager to see him as he is to see her, because she arrives early, too.

Marty says quietly, "Hi, Nikki baby."

Nikki says, "I love you. How are you?"

Marty says, "When I'm with you it's heaven. I'm happy."

"Me too. What's happening? I want to know."

"Oh, the job is the same old stuff, another day at Elastics and Plastics. And you know, every night with Natalie—well, I might as well still be at E&P. You know what I mean. You know how Natalie is. Same old, same old."

"Yes, you're bigger than all that. You have so much more to offer. You're beyond that," Nikki says softly, leaning her head toward Marty.

"It's true. I've become somebody totally different and she's still the same."

It's four o'clock on a Friday afternoon and Curt and Julie walk out of a required company mission statement meeting, realizing that the meeting ended an hour early.

"Yeah, those guys from headquarters want to leave early for the weekend too," Curt says.

"I'm just glad we're finished. Want to stop for a drink?" Julie asks.

"Why not? I'm in no hurry to get home," Curt says.

As they sit down at a small table in the Whistle and Bull Bar, Curt asks Julie, "Are you still seeing Mark?"

"Yes, I am," Julie says, "we're made for each other. We're in love and we're both growing."

"That's wonderful. Wish I could say the same. But there's only one person growing in my house and it's not Susie. It's obvious. I've grown and she hasn't. It's the sadness of our marriage."

He's talking to A BMW (Anyone But My Wife). Everyone else seems more supportive and understanding to our man. This is not surprising. A BMW doesn't have the information to know that almost everything he's saying has no basis in fact. The natural reaction of a listener is to accept everything he's saying as the absolute truth. Why would one doubt the accuracy of what he says about a person he knows so well, especially since the characteristics he is choosing to comment on seem so big and deep, so spiritual and high-minded, not small or petty or base like dress, weight, or the way she keeps house. He is unconsciously following the Script's instructions to start developing his character as a positive, high-minded, thoughtful man always striving for the loftiest ideals.

The stranger also finds it easier to listen because the commentary is about someone else. Our man is commenting on and implicitly criticizing and belittling someone else, his wife. If he said it directly to his wife she might take it as an attack and might counter-attack. The stranger or work colleague is a safe person with whom he can test out his feelings.

A BMW also feels complimented to be the one he chooses to confide in and may be eager to share in the most personal details of someone else's life.

"Hey, Nelson, how's it going?" Larry says as he runs into Nelson walking into the Power-Up Gym one Thursday morning at 6:00 A.M. Nelson answers, "Goin' great. What about you, big guy? You're sure lookin' trim."

"Yeah, I'm working at it. Doin' the treadmill this morning?"

"Yes I am. You too?"

"Yup, meet you there."

Larry and Nelson spend an intense hour on the treadmill, each one comparing his incline setting to the other's and both trying to go as steeply as they can.

They're off to the locker room at 7:00 A.M. and as they're toweling off after showering, Larry says to Nelson, "How's Katrina and the kids?"

Nelson answers, "The kids are great. Only thing is with Katrina, I'm here at six o'clock every morning and she's still home fiddling in the kitchen. I told her, 'Come with me, you'll be toned and trim.' She says no. I told her, 'If you come with me I'll go to the gym after work instead of before.' But she says no, it's just not something she would enjoy doing. So she comes once a month for half an hour."

Larry says, "I guess she's just not going to be working out." Larry pauses as he realizes how that sounded and says, "Oh, I didn't mean it that way."

"No, listen, I've thought about it that way too," Nelson says. "She just doesn't do the stuff I want her to do."

For once Peggy and Hal have an uncommitted Sunday morning and are sitting on their deck relaxing with the Sunday paper when Hal says, "Did you see that about Trisphere's stock going through the roof?"

"Yes, I saw the headline," Peggy says.

"That's all you read was the headline? It's a big deal," Hal says.

"I was reading something else," Peggy replies.

"Aren't you interested in the stock market? You don't seem interested in anything that I am. You're not interested in computers, you're not interested in the stock market, you're not interested in racing our sailboat. We no longer have anything to talk about."

"I wouldn't say that. We have the family, travel, just everything we do every day."

"No, Peggy. I've grown and you haven't. You just don't understand me."

TIP: EUREKA! HE'S SPEAKING!

Eureka! He's speaking! To you! And the words are not about sports, not about his job, not about the kids, not about the house, not really about the stock market. They're about how he feels! Maybe he's trying to communicate.

Yes, what he's saying is hurtful, insulting, critical, short-tempered. (And worse, you may find out later he was saying some of these same things behind your back to others.)

It's hard to listen to sentiments like this and even harder to continue the conversation without being hurtful, insulting, critical, or short-tempered in response. But if he is speaking about how he feels, listen and encourage him to talk further. Maybe your encouraging response will lead to more conversation and he will see that he really *does* have someone who understands him.

Signals

If there's nothing to talk about, there's a lot to talk about. It's hard to pick up the weak signal he has sent that says he wants to talk, especially since it was accompanied by a lot of disturbing static. But we hope that by now you know the code words he's likely to use in this scene, and you will be able to decipher the signal better and not inadvertently cut off a chance to communicate.

- We've grown apart.

- I've become somebody totally different and
  you're still the same.

- I've grown and she hasn't. It's the sadness of
  our marriage.

- She just doesn't do the stuff I want her to do.

- You just don't understand me.

All signals mean something, and it's usually good to listen.

SCENE 6: "I FOUND MY SOUL MATE"

Tim had been training for the triathlon for six months. His endurance skills were turning out to be stronger than he'd thought they'd be. He was comparing very favorably to men twenty years younger who were doing the training with him every weekend. And from the beginning he had hit it off with the training assistant, Debbie. She told him he was really looking good to win the meet for men forty and over.

Sometimes he would sit with Debbie during the energy breaks and they swapped stories of sports events they'd participated in.

Once, after the Saturday training was finished, Debbie invited him to her apartment to see some special training videos. Debbie changed from the shorts and tank top she wore for the training to a sundress and sandals. After watching the videos, Tim said he'd better be on his way home. Debbie gave him a quick squeeze good-bye and wished him a good Saturday evening with his family.

More and more of Tim's Saturday afternoons ended at Debbie's apartment. She always chose Tim to pass her special training tips on to. Once she invited him over to give him a hat and t-shirt the race sponsor had provided for the most motivated competitor. Debbie asked about Tim's wife from time to time. At first Tim said nothing. Then one evening when they were sitting on the sofa, Tim told Debbie that he and his wife had really grown apart. His wife seemed to be so preoccupied with the house and the kids that she hardly paid any attention to him. Debbie moved closer to him on the sofa and Tim moved closer still until they were embracing. That first night they stopped at one passionate kiss. The following Saturday, they went further. They never actually slept together. They did everything but.

Tim started to stay later and later at Debbie's on Saturday evenings. He told his wife that as it got nearer to the meet, the training sessions were lasting longer and longer.

Later and later meant closer and closer. Soon Tim saw that he couldn't live without Saturday nights at Debbie's. Not only couldn't he live without Saturday nights at Debbie's, he couldn't live without living with her. Debbie found him so attractive, she was so good to him, she was so alluring. "She makes me happy," he thought. "I found my soul mate."

He's found his soul mate and he's truly happy. But he realizes that to have enough time to experience this happiness he has to cover all his bases—including home base. There can't be any questions about why he is spending so much time on third.

Karen has just finished with the kids, the kitchen, and the nonstop phone calls, and has settled in front of the TV for a little rest to

wait until Gil comes home. She looks at her watch—10:30 P.M.—
and thinks he's later than he said he would be when she hears his
footsteps.

"Gosh, you worked late tonight, honey," Karen says.

"Yes, sorry to be home so late, but when you hear why you're
gonna be thrilled. This big deal is coming down the pike and it's
going to be huge, I mean huge. We're going to be rolling in it, I
mean we're gonna have so many of the things you want, I can
hardly tell you. But you gotta stay with me on this. Getting the
deal done is going to take a lot of time. I'm gonna come home
late more than once. And I'm gonna be tired a lot. Are you with
me on this?"

"Sure, honey. Just what we always dreamed about. That's wonderful. I can live with the rest for the time being. When do you
think it will be done?"

"Hard to say. It could take a while. You gotta stay with me on
this."

An ounce of preparation is worth a pound of explanation. He
doesn't have a deal at all. He's making it up. The Script has taught
him to prepare. Set up the next scenes in advance, the Script has
told him. Buy some stress-free time, get the lead actress on board
with your (cover) story line. And turn her head away from the real
plot. You will be free of her uncomfortable questions for a comfortable period of time. She will be thinking about how hard
you're working and how late you're working and the pot of gold
you've promised at the end. Her attention will be completely di-
verted from the place you don't want her to look.

SCENE 7: "THIS COULD WORK"

Don is a lucky man. He has a mistress, Tammy, who makes him feel so happy. He has a wife, Ella, who makes him feel so comfortable. He has his children, who make him feel so proud, and he has his job, which makes him feel so powerful. He can have it all—the comfort and respect of his wife and family and the happy, alive, desirable, admired feeling Tammy brings him. "I feel so happy. Everybody is happy. This feeling can last forever."

He is in a delusional state, living in a fantasy. The world full of possibilities has produced one wonderful woman, his soul mate. He feels happy, alive, appreciated, on top of the world. The thought of hurt, angry, scared, disapproving, or suddenly distant family and friends is absolutely nowhere in his mind.

At first, he just wants things to continue like this. Some men want to stay at this stage, with a wife *and* a girlfriend. Others begin to think naturally of marrying their "soul mate." Others move in that direction due to pressure from the girlfriend (see Scene 8).

Practical problems of money, where everyone will live, and the children's future figure nowhere in his vision. His fantasies will play out like this: "Look at Joe. He just moved in with Kathy. He's so happy. His wife is getting along fine and his kids are doing great, Joe said. He sees his kids every other weekend and Joe said he just took the whole gang—his three kids and Kathy—to Miami. The kids love Kathy and she's great with them. She fits right into their life and she's so patient with them. Joe's wife, she's just doing her thing as always, not causing him any problems. Whatever he says she goes along with. She always was a plain, simple woman who could roll with the punches. Yeah, well, that's one reason he obviously had to leave her—with her figure, she could roll a little too easily."

"This could work—I can keep everybody happy" is the fantasy he is living now. It is extremely difficult for anyone to comprehend how he could be so delusional. But it's all part of the Script.

SCENE 8: "THIS ISN'T FAIR"

Lulu and Ed are finishing dinner on the balcony off Lulu's apartment.

LULU: Can I start to make some plans now? We've been talking about getting married for so long.

ED: Not just yet. Soon, though.

LULU: Soon when? First you have to tell Margaret. When are you going to tell her you want a divorce?

ED: I will, I will. I love you, baby. We're gonna be together. Don't worry.

LULU: I love you too. That's why we need to get married. And I've been waiting and waiting.

Ed walks into his house at ten o'clock at night. Margaret's been waiting since dinnertime for him to come home but she figured it must be another one of those end-of-the-quarter, last-push sales meetings that was keeping him at the office. But when Ed walks in she isn't so sure. He doesn't have his laptop briefcase with him and he doesn't look that tired. Ed had admitted that he had had a couple of dinners that lasted late with that woman in his office. Margaret accused him of sleeping with her but Ed denied it. But now Margaret has a feeling Ed spent this evening in bed with that overdone slut. So, fed up with his philandering, she snaps. "Where were you?" she yells at Ed. "With that evil, pushy bitch, were you? I'm telling you, stop seeing her or get out of the house. What do you think I am, a doormat?"

Ed says, "Calm down. I'm home, right? What do you want? We're going out for dinner tomorrow, aren't we? I planned a really nice evening for you."

Margaret replies, "If you're seeing that woman, stop. Otherwise I don't want you in the house."

Ed doesn't know why everyone's so angry and upset with him. Everything was going so well. Why is Lulu pressuring him so much to get married? He's been so good to her. And what is Margaret complaining about? Her life hasn't changed. She's still going out with her friends and doing things with the kids. Just what she likes. She has everything she could ever want.

"Gosh, don't people appreciate what I've done for them? Let everything be. It's fine. I'm outraged."

"This isn't fair."

SCENE 9: MONEY TALKS . . . IT ALSO FOLLOWS THE SCRIPT

He doesn't have a large speaking part in this scene, but Money does. And you're listening. Even though he tries to make you think you're hearing things, we can tell you your reception is excellent. Here's how the Script goes, as Money enters devilishly from a trapdoor below stage, decked in his time-honored green costume.

WIFE: What's all that cash you have stuffed in your wallet on the dresser?

HUSBAND: What cash?

WIFE: You must have a couple thousand dollars stuffed in your wallet. It's going to burst. What do you need all that cash for?

HUSBAND: It's not a lot of cash. I just need it when I'm traveling to the different offices. I can't be running to the ATM all the time.

Lots of cash around. You're not imagining it—you really are hearing an unusual number of hundred-dollar bills rustling against each other. That money is really talking. The rustling sound is telling you these bills have left the bank account to be used for gifts, restaurants, hotels, and other infidelity expenses. This cash is making very audible rustling noises now but it's going to start talking a lot more quietly because it doesn't want to be traced. He's gone to using cash because expenses paid in cash are harder to trace—no credit card statements and no cancelled checks.

On the other hand, you might find that suddenly he's spending too *little.*

WIFE: I was looking at the bank account. You're not taking much money out of the ATM the last few months. How are you managing?

HUSBAND: I'm managing the same as I always did.

WIFE: Are you putting some stuff on the credit cards?

HUSBAND: Yes, some of it.

WIFE: I don't see that the credit card bills are higher.

HUSBAND: I don't know what you're seeing, but you're not seeing straight. Quit the third degree. Don't you have anything else to do?

You're not imagining the whisper-soft sounds of Money talking here. It's quiet but not silent. It's saying to you, "I feel unused. How come he's not spending me?"

He's gone to spending less because he can't be seen out and about. He has to stay inside, usually at her house or a secret, out-of-the-way location they've discovered. Staying in means spending less because eating at home costs less than eating in a restaurant. Watching a video costs less than tickets purchased under the bright lights of a movie marquee.

Spending too much, especially cash, or spending too little. He's not talking but Money is, and your understanding of Money's language is exactly right even though he's trying to tell you you're hearing things.

TIP: WHEN MONEY TALKS IT
SPEAKS THE TRUTH.

Money feeling especially used or unused will let you know.

SCENE 10: GETTING HIS DUCKS IN A ROW

Ray is sitting in his office mulling over his evening with Steph two nights earlier. "Yes, she makes me feel so alive, so happy," he thinks. "I've got to be with her. Everything will work out fine with Libby and the kids. They'll manage on their own. I'll have a wonderful life with Steph."

"Steph, don't worry," Ray says as he talks to her from his office right before he leaves for the day.

Steph had been asking Ray how his mother would react to her. And what about his kids? How would they take to another mother?

"The kids will take to you from the get-go. My mom too. You've got a warm way with everybody. They're gonna love you."

.   .   .

Ray is thinking, "It'll work out great to move into Steph's condo. I already feel like I live there. More than just live there really—I feel *alive* there. It's smaller than the house I have now, but who cares."

Ron is walking down Michigan Avenue on his way to lunch. It's a windy, cold day. He wants to get to the restaurant as soon as possible, but he can't help stopping for a minute when a huge sign in the window of Elephant Investments catches his eye. "Bring your IRA Rollover to Elephant. Gigantic choice of investments including hedge funds." Ron thinks, "That's a great idea. I want to get into hedge funds. I've got $225,000 in my IRA. That's mine. When I move the account I'll change the address so the statement comes to the office. Jennifer doesn't even have to know about that. She probably doesn't pay any attention to the retirement accounts anyway."

Marc comes down the stairs with his keys in his hand. "Hey, Ginnie, I know it's Saturday but I have to run to the office. The big guy just called another urgent meeting. I'll be back as soon as I can. Probably a couple of hours."

Ginnie looks up from loading the dishwasher. "Okay. Come back soon. There's lots to do. It's Saturday."

Marc pulls out of the driveway and turns left in the direction of his office. But two minutes later, when he is out of sight of the house, he doubles back because Kiki's apartment is really in the opposite direction.

Driving to Kiki's he thinks about when he'll be able to move in with her. "As soon as I find the right time to tell Ginnie, I'm going to let her know it's over. It'll be so exciting living with Kiki. She loves to do all the things I like to do. None of the burdensome stuff I have on my plate now. Ginnie will remarry. I know it. She won't want to be alone. She'll find somebody. He'll take care of her. I'll be free of that burden."

He has everything set in his mind. All will go beautifully. He is mentally imagining how he will drop the Bomb and how wonderful his life will be after that. He will continue to have it all. He is still in the delusional fantasy period, so he has no thoughts of problems regarding living arrangements, his children's needs, or how everyone will get along. But he does realize that having it all after he drops the Bomb will involve some planning. He may have started to hide money quite a while ago, when he first began to create a cover story. If not, we can predict he will start to hide money now or in the near future.

"Nick, here's five thousand dollars for each of the kids to add to their college accounts," Nick's mother says to him as she hands him two checks. "I want to do this for the kids and I have the money. You and Sharon go put this in their college savings accounts at the bank."

"Oh, thanks, Mom," Nick says. "That's really nice."

Driving home from his mother's house, Nick has an even better idea. He thinks, "College is a long time away and who knows if the kids will even go to college. Anyway, they can start at the community college. It's really inexpensive. They wouldn't need close to five grand. I'm going to put that in the account I just opened at Valley Trust Bank. Mom really meant to help me anyway."

. . .

It seems hard to believe that a man would divert money intended for his own children, but in the fantasy period some fathers do just that. From listening to other men act out the Script our man has learned how to get things done secretly and he has rehearsed some excellent personal and public explanations for his behavior, should he need them. He plans to have it all and knows this will involve some undercover work.

Phil and Rick are having a drink in Grand Central Station before catching the train home to Rye. Rick listens as Phil says, "Yeah, I'm living with Jill now. Got the house sold. Jill and I are buying a place at Harbor Point. It's the top floor unit with the wraparound terrace and the private boat dock. Tessie and the kids don't need that big house on Magnolia Lane. I told her a year ago—'Get this place spruced up.' I wanted to sell it quickly and I did. Now I'm all set. I feel young again."

Rick thinks to himself, "Phil really knows how to get things done. One, two, three, he's rid of that sourpuss. And he has a new life."

"What kind of paycheck do you think you'll get for April?" Carol asks her husband, Walt. "I thought we could finally get some new carpet in the family room."

"I don't know. Not so good. Sales were down. Nobody's buying new cars these days. I'm not going to get any more than my base. I'm doing my best but nobody's biting," Walt replies.

"Oh gosh. I guess we're not getting new carpet this month," Carol says.

Later Carol remembers seeing a printout on Walt's desk that said new car sales were up in his region. She says to Walt, "I saw the printout on your desk in the den that said sales were up in your group. How come yours were down?"

Walt answers, "That printout was about something totally different. Don't you think I'm telling you the truth? Do you think you know everything about all the group sales just from reading one printout?"

Carol answers, "No, I don't think I know everything about the group's sales, but it just seemed strange that yours were so different."

"Hey, Beth, you've got to get this spare bedroom cleaned up. What if we wanted to sell the house? Nobody would want it with all this junk in here," Rod says.

"Okay, okay," Beth answers. "I know it's piled high. I just haven't had a chance to get to it. But anyway, what's the rush? Who's talking about selling the house?"

Rod realizes he may have said a little too much, but he covers quickly when he says, "You never know. Look at the Rinewalds. All of a sudden he was transferred."

Todd is driving back to his office after showing a new line of adhesives to the purchasing manager at Mountain Industries' distant plant. It's getting dark and his mind starts to wander from business to planning for his new life with Celine. He thinks, "I've got to streamline all the heavy expenses with Dottie. For sure, we'll sell the house. What does she need such a big house for? She won't even want it. She doesn't need anything fancy. Something much smaller will do her fine. I'm going to talk to that agent that Mike used. She got his house sold really quickly and for a good price. I want to find out what we can get for ours. I'm going to tell the agent not to even mention it to Dottie. Let the agent just drive by and tell me what it's worth." Yes, Todd is secretly getting all his ducks in a row.

As he's lining up his ducks, he does as much of his work undercover as he can, keeping his strategies secret from everyone. Some thinking and planning about how things will line up after he drops the Bomb is going on silently in his head. But some of his planning is visible to the naked eye. You notice some kind of change. You may ask him about it. The explanation he gives you seems reasonable, and there is no reason not to believe what he's telling you. So you see the ducks but there doesn't seem to be any reason to look under their wings.

Ella is dusting the books and Don's collection of signed baseballs in the den when she sees that the shelf that always had the signed balls from the Boston Red Sox looks a little bare. "I know he always had that ball signed by Ted Williams and the one from Carl Yastrzemski and the one from Roger Clemens. Don prized those balls. Did I put them somewhere else or did Don put them on another shelf?" she wonders. She looks all over the den and can't find them and figures that Don put them somewhere and didn't tell her.

"Hey, Greta," Ben says, "I see you're spending a lot of time on the books for the business. I've been thinking about it for a while. I'm going to hire a bookkeeper so you don't have to work so hard. You know business is going to be up this spring and summer. I already have signed contracts for four big homes, plus there are some really solid leads in the pipeline. It's going to be too much for you."

Greta has been doing the books for Ben's home contracting business for almost six years. It's a lot of work. She's thrilled to hear Ben's idea. "I know we always wanted to save the money for ourselves instead of putting it to a bookkeeper's salary," she says, "but I think you're right. It's getting to be too much for me and with all the paperwork from four new projects it'll be overwhelming. I really do think you should find someone."

Ben immediately hires a bookkeeper and after the new hire has been on the job for a few weeks, Greta thinks back over the amounts the bookkeeper has been depositing into their household account each week. The deposits seem to be no more than last year's income and maybe a little bit less.

When Ben comes home that night she asks him, "Is the bookkeeper getting things right? I looked at the deposits into our household account from the business and they're actually lower than last year even though you said they were going to be more."

Ben says, "She's doing a great job. Don't you even be thinking about it. That's exactly what I meant—this is just too involved for you now. With all these houses I'm doing, expenses are just going to be higher."

"Okay. I still don't quite understand why the deposits are lower but I guess you know what you're doing."

One day Karen sees her husband, Gil, carrying all his elaborate audio equipment up from the basement. She asks him, "Gil, what are you doing?"

Gil answers, "I'm selling everything. Who needs all this stuff? I'm keeping one turntable and that's it."

Karen can't quite figure out why Gil would all of a sudden decide to sell the audio equipment he loved so much. She says, "Just like that you're selling everything? You always said that only a child could live without a whole setup."

"Well, that's it," he says. "I already have someone to buy it all."

A week later Karen starts wondering how much Gil got for all the equipment that cost so much when he bought it. She asks him. "What did all that stuff bring when you sold it?"

Gil says, "Oh, not that much. The guy who bought it is going to send me a check."

In fact, Gil has already gotten his money—almost five thousand dollars—which he has stashed in an envelope in his desk in the basement.

When Ron moved his IRA to Elephant Investments and changed the statement address to his office, he was hoping that Jennifer wouldn't even notice. Then she would lose track of that asset altogether.

Nick sees an opportunity to put a little money aside for himself when his mother gives him the checks intended for his children's college education. And Walt has a special opportunity to put money away from anyone else's eyes because Carol would find it difficult and awkward to find out exactly what Walt's sales and commissions really were.

Ben has engaged in some extra work and planning—going to the trouble of hiring a bookkeeper—because, his thinking goes, "If

Greta doesn't see the books she will never really know exactly what should be coming into the household account." He can take some of the revenue and put it to his own ends.

Don sees a source of ready cash in his baseball collectibles and sells them without telling anybody.

He has it all sorted out in his head, and as much as he can accomplish secretly, in the bank. He's got his ducks in a row.

TIP: DUCKS DON'T KEEP SECRETS

These ducks are quacking and flapping their wings. You've noticed it but it's very natural for ducks to quack and flap their wings. So you ignore the ducks. But when the quacking comes with a nervous, unnatural edge and the flapping creates ripples of unease and there's no explanation, you have to listen to the ducks. Because ducks don't keep secrets.

Keep an eye on the assets you have such as bank accounts, investments, your home, paychecks, valuables, and credit cards. Continue keeping your journal recording each time a duck quacks. If he is planning to leave, your knowledge of the finances will help you. You don't want to be forced to hire an investigator who will have to start from scratch, looking for clues as to where the money has gone.

If It's Too Bad to Be True, Unfortunately, It Probably Is

If it's too bad to be true, unfortunately, it probably is.

In other words, if you have a feeling that something isn't right, it probably isn't.

The truth is *most* men tend to be secretive about things because that's the way they've learned to play life's games. So the fact that a man is secretive doesn't prove anything. What does mean something is the feeling you have.

It's very hard to confront him when something doesn't seem right. If, in fact, things aren't all right, the impact on you and your family will be frightful. You know this and try to find reasonable explanations for the questions you have in your head. In the end, though, you have to listen to the ducks.

SCENE 11: THE EXPENSIVE GIFT

Wendy hears Howie's car pull into the garage a little earlier than usual and turns to the oven to get the lasagna on the table. She expects to hear Howie open the door into the house in a second but instead she hears rustling noises coming from the garage. A minute later Howie comes in.

"Hi, honey. I brought you something," he says.

"Ooh, what's that? Oh, my gosh, from Sophia di Milano. What is it?"

"Here, it's for you."

Wendy takes the large box and sets it on the table to open it. She pulls aside the fancy tissue paper with Sophia di Milano written all over it to reveal a gorgeous lilac suit with the most beautiful buttons she has ever seen.

"Oh, Howie," Wendy says. "You bought this for me? From Sophia di Milano? I've never had anything from such an expensive store. I love it. I can wear it on Friday to the reception."

Wendy thinks, "My goodness, Howie went so far from his office to go to Sophia di Milano. He chose a store he knew would just thrill me. And he picked such a beautiful suit. Yes, Howie just shuts me out at times but then look how he makes it up to me."

"I think I'm about ready to crawl into bed. It's past eleven o'clock," Emily says to her husband.

Joe responds, "I'll run up and start getting ready. I'm ready to turn in too."

Emily says "Fine," and follows a couple of minutes later.

Upstairs in the bedroom as Emily goes to turn down the comforter, she sees a beautiful silver box with a huge gold bow on her pillow. "What's this?" she asks Joe.

Joe says, "Open it."

Emily thinks, "It's not my birthday, it's not our anniversary, it's not Mother's Day. What is this?" She pulls off the bow, opens the box, sees a gorgeous blue cashmere sweater. "Oooh, Joe, this is beautiful. Thank you."

"Put it on," Joe says.

As Emily slowly puts it on she thinks, "Gosh, Joe hasn't done anything like this in a long time. And he never took the time to go to the mall to buy me a gift. It's so expensive, so soft. He must still think of me as sexy and attractive and number one. And here I had been thinking he might be interested in other women because he seemed to be looking everywhere but at me."

"Rita, a brand new Escalade? Gosh, it's gorgeous. Did you just get it?" Carol asks.

"Yes, I love it. Chuck gave it to me. He said he wanted me to have a new car. Chuck's never bought me anything like this before," Rita says.

Carol thinks to herself, "Gee, I wish Marty would buy me a car like that. But I have to say all in all Chuck isn't the kindest, warmest husband in the world. He's always got his head off somewhere else when Marty and I see him and Rita. But he sure came through this time to express his feelings for Rita. Deep down he must be a really good guy."

Two months later Carol hears that Chuck and Rita are getting divorced. She thinks back to how ecstatic Rita had seemed not that long ago when she was talking about the expensive car Chuck had given her. Carol wonders why a man would go out of his way to spend so much money on a gift for his wife right before he tells her he doesn't love her.

You think:

A gift so beautifully packaged and presented could only have one meaning—"I really, really love you."

A gift given "just because" could only have one meaning—"I really, really love you."

A gift far more expensive than one my husband ever, ever bought me could only have one meaning—"I really, really love you."

A gift requiring so much planning and effort to purchase could only have one meaning—"I really, really love you."

It's natural and good for any woman to have this feeling upon receiving an expensive gift. And yes, it may mean just that—we hope it does. But if this is *the* Expensive Gift and he has been playing through the first scenes of the Script, this gift may come with strings attached. The strings lead to other reasons a man might give his wife an unusually expensive gift. This gift may be:

The Guilty Gift—He may be feeling guilty for having been distant and cold to you recently, for having paid little attention to you, and for another relationship that he knows has gone too far. He is giving you this gift to assuage his guilt. "Please don't make me feel guilty," the attached string says.

The "See, I'm a Really Good Guy" Gift—He thinks that neither you nor the world could possibly think ill of a man who has been so incredibly generous to his wife . . . no matter what happens in the future. "Please think of me as a really good guy and when you speak of me, please tell the world I'm a really good person," the attached string says.

The "This Will Prevent You from Ever Being Angry with Me" Gift—If he has been following the Script through Act I, the Expensive Gift is excellent preparation for Act II. He knows your anger will be coming at some point after he drops the Bomb. "You see how much I want you to be contented. You cannot get angry with someone so concerned with your well-being," the attached string says.

The "I'm Going to Lead Her Off the Scent" Gift—If he wants to distract you from following any clues linking him to the crime scene, giving you a spectacular, attention-getting gift turns your thoughts to his love and concern for you. "Look this way, look this way, don't look over there," the attached string says.

"I haven't been paying much attention to Julie lately," Tim thinks. "It seems like she's kind of cold to me too. It couldn't be that she's suspicious, could it? I know what. I'm going to buy her those diamond earrings she's been hinting at for so long. That'll warm her up and calm her down and turn her in the right direction. She'll be looking lovingly at me and at the earrings. She won't even think to look anywhere else. Regardless of what happens, she'll always regard me as the good, generous guy. She could never be angry with me. She'll always think I'm so giving."

TIP: LOOK A GIFT HORSE IN THE MOUTH

Sometimes you *do* have to look a gift horse in the mouth. In the eyes too. You have to ask yourself, "Has this gift horse been mouthing 'Neigh, neigh' while trying to get me to say 'Yay, yay?'" Then this gift may not have come from a place of love and caring.

You have to ask yourself, "What has been the general atmosphere on the ranch?" In thinking back, you may see that he has been somewhat distant recently and less interested in you and your life. Even in the face of this evidence, it's easier to just be grateful. It's more in tune with the way you've always thought about him and more

in tune with the way you've been taught to think about
people in general—Think the best of everyone—to think
of the expensive gift as a gesture of love. It's easy to for-
get the second part of that directive: plan for the worst.

It *is* natural to think that your husband would only give
you a gift like this for the most loving and generous of
reasons. "Don't look a gift horse in the mouth" is the old
adage. But sometimes you do have to look a gift horse in
the mouth. It depends on the general atmosphere on the
ranch and whether you've heard any other lines of the
Script.

A Word to the Guys

*Listen up because this is the first, last, and only word to the wise we're
gonna give you.*

*The game is up because the book is out. Through Act I you've always had
a free ride because nobody could decipher your signals. But from the day
this book is published going forward it's going to be a little bit easier to
understand what you're thinking. We know that not all of you who act
out the drama of the first act are being unfaithful. Thinking is not doing.
No harm in having a little fun in thinking either.*

*But when you start speaking your lines in Act II, the free ride is over.
Thanks to The Script, every woman will know exactly what you're up
to.*

*So, we say to you, a little drama in one's life can be fun. But look before
you leap because this drama can also do lasting damage. (See the finale:
This Is Not the Way I Planned It.)*

TIP (FOR THE WOMEN): GO SLOWLY AND ALL SHALL BE REVEALED TO YOU

Contain your anxiety, because being anxious will not help you to influence the future.

You can't reason with him now, and you can't control what he is doing and thinking. You can't really understand it either; nobody can. That's because you are in the real world while he may be in another world, a fantasy world.

And remember that if you sense that the man you're with, or a man you know, is doing or thinking some of the things at the beginning of this act, it does *not* mean that all these men are cheating.

If the facts are still not clear, keep reading. The Script you will see unfold before you will help you to know if he is just thinking about having an affair—or actually *doing* it.

ACT II

AFTER HE LEAVES

The curtain is about to rise on Act II. The stagehands breathe easier because they will have a break from the very tense and tight scene changes they had in Act I. The director had warned them before Act I that the tiniest mistake removing props when the curtain came down on a scene could cause the entire play to go haywire. Likewise, the director said, using the wrong props to set up for a new scene could cause one of the actresses to walk off the stage.

As the audience takes a break during intermission, the stagehands are hurrying to dismantle the screen that divided the stage into two separate sets for Act I. The director can relax a little in Act II because he won't have to worry about the male lead flubbing the complicated exits and entrances the two sets entailed. The lighting technicians prepare to shine the spotlight on the leading actress throughout this act. The audience will be able to observe her reaction as a supporting actress, formerly hidden by the screen, brazenly tries to upstage her.

The curtain rises on Act II and the orchestra conductor points his baton at the percussionist. The cymbals come together with a resounding crash. The male lead enters from stage right and we see him Dropping the Bomb.

SCENE 1: DROPPING THE BOMB

The whole Reed family is at the Princess Royal Hotel in Barbados—Jeff, Amy, nine-year-old Jeffrey Jr., six-year-old Matthew, Jeff's parents, and Amy's mother, Martha. Jeff wanted everyone together for this long-anticipated vacation at the newest and most luxurious hotel in Barbados. He had worked hard planning every detail for his family.

Now, the morning of the last day comes and Jeff tells Amy to invite everyone to their cottage for a 5:00 P.M. drink before dinner, right after the boys get back from swimming. Amy had been thinking of relaxing before dinner and going for a late romantic table for two at nine. But she wants to make Jeff happy, so she calls all the grandparents and asks them to come at five.

The elder Reeds and Amy's mother are all sitting down with a drink while the boys quiet down with a Coke. Amy comes in from the bedroom dressed in her gorgeous new cocktail dress and Jeff hands her a glass of Chardonnay, her favorite. Jeff's mother raises her glass in a toast. "Thank you, Jeff, for a wonderful vacation. It was great to all be together. Are my grandsons something else or what?"

"I'm glad you enjoyed it, Mom. Guys, I wanted to make everything nice for you all. Most of all I want the best for my family," Jeff says. "So, boys, everything will be okay. And Mom and Dad and Martha, don't you worry. Amy and I are splitting up. It'll all be the same as it's always been. We're a family."

One of Detroit's most glittering social events, celebrating the debut of the daughter of its most famous family, is taking place in a glorious setting. No expense has been spared to make it the most sumptuous and magnificent celebration possible. Anne Ford, the nineteen-year-old daughter of Anne and Henry Ford II, the chairman of Ford Motor Company and grandson of the founder of one of the world's largest and best-known companies, will be making her official entrance into society.

As the extravagant food and entertainment continue throughout the evening, none of the guests has any idea of the hurt and devastation occupying the hearts and minds of the debutante, her mother, her sister Charlotte, and her brother Edsel, because they are concealing it so well.

However, the night before this society spectacular, Henry Ford II had announced to his family that he was leaving his wife of twenty-three years.

It's incomprehensible to you. How could he choose exactly the occasion when the family is closest together, the occasion that had required so much planning, that had created so much excited anticipation, the occasion where you have no place to hide and no place to react in private, the occasion that intensifies the hurt, the most inappropriate situation of all?

Dropping the Bomb in an unbelievably inappropriate setting is not always part of the Script, but it's amazing how many times it is. It leaves everyone completely baffled and silent. As the news sinks in, they're also very angry: just the result he intended. He's probably ambivalent about leaving, but now that he's made the intensely hurtful also intensely outrageous, it can only go one way. He's leaving and that's final. No discussion, no explanation, no begging, no counseling, no emotion from the family. They're too shocked and angry even to speak.

Twenty-three members of the Cressman family have gathered for Thanksgiving dinner this year. Susie and Ned, their three children—fourteen-year-old Jenny, twelve-year-old Zach, and eight-year-old Crissy—grandmothers, aunts, uncles, cousins, and even an elderly neighbor. The turkey is ready and the squash soup too. Susie calls to her son, Zach, to ask if everyone is sitting down. Zach answers, "Yes, everyone but Dad." Susie tells Zach that Dad went out to buy some beer he said he had to have for Thanksgiving but that he should be back soon. Susie carries the special antique soup tureen they use just twice a year into the dining room and sits down in her appointed chair to wait for Ned.

Just then Susie hears the garage door opening and Ned walking in. She calls out to Ned that she's just about to ladle out the soup and please hurry and sit down. Ned walks into the dining room holding the hand of a strange woman. He sets the imported beer down on the sideboard and says, "Hi, everyone. This is my girl-friend, Allison. I'm leaving you, Susie, and came to get my things. Allison and I are going away for a while. Enjoy the beer." Ned grabs a packed satchel from a closet and rushes out.

Everyone sits stunned as the door to the garage shuts behind him and they hear the car drive away.

For twenty years the entire Guilford family had gone to St. Bart's for two weeks at Christmas—Max, Helena, and the four children. They went even before Max and Helena *had* children. This year was more fun than ever. The kids were old enough now to enjoy sailing and snorkeling and water skiing and to take care of themselves. Max and Helena had time to spend alone together. Helena found it so relaxing that she suggested to Max that they buy a second home there. Max said, "Good idea."

But now the two weeks are over and they all pile into the hotel limo to go to the airport to fly home. They are waiting in line to board the plane when all of a sudden Max says to his family, "I'm not getting on the plane with you to go back to Chicago. I'm leaving you, Helena."

It is the evening of Mindy's special birthday dinner and she and Charlie walk up to their candlelit table and twenty-five invited friends in the most beautiful French restaurant in Atlanta. They eat and laugh and laugh some more, until they have finished the main course and two waiters come in carrying a cake ablaze with candles.

Mindy is so happy. She makes a wish, blows out the candles, and is basking in the romantic spotlight when a strange man pushes his way to the table and slaps some papers into her hand. Charlie sees that the process server has completed his job and says to Mindy, "I'm divorcing you, you bitch."

Everyone sits in stunned silence, totally confused by what just happened.

If the setting is not outrageous and precisely a symbol of what he is about to destroy—family togetherness, romance, love—then the words he uses to accompany the Bomb will represent these ideals.

Derek leaves very early for work. Cece wonders why he's been leaving so early over the past few months. But she knows Derek likes to get an early start before the phones start ringing and people interrupt him, so it seems to make sense. She knows he hates a lot of questions so she doesn't ask.

Around 10:00 A.M. Derek calls to say he's coming home from work. He's only fifteen minutes away.

"Are you sick?" Cece asks. "You don't sound good."

"No, I'm not sick," Derek responds.

"Okay, I'll see you in a few minutes then. You really don't sound right."

Fifteen minutes later, Derek arrives home and says abruptly to Cece, "I can't live like this anymore."

"What do you mean?" Cece is shocked.

"I want a divorce."

Derek tells Cece that he had considered divorce a few years before, but he waited because she had had health problems at the time. Yes, Derek was really thinking of her welfare. But he was preparing for himself, too, because he had seen a lawyer more than a year earlier.

Being solicitous of his wife's health, not wanting to hurt her just when she's coping with a serious illness—these are laudable values that appear to show caring, self-restraint, and selflessness. You can't argue with that. Which is exactly what he wants.

If you disagree with these admirable, praiseworthy, and religiously endorsed values you seem ungrateful, ignorant, critical, unloving, and distant. But you know you can't agree with what he's said because, even in your state of shock, you realize that there's something not right about pairing caring, self-restraint, and selflessness with leaving your family.

There is nothing you can say. Which is exactly what he wants.

. . .

It is quieter than the usual Sunday morning when Heather and Mark sit down to brunch because the kids are sleeping over at Grandma's. Heather is restfully sipping her coffee when Mark says, "You know, Heather, there has never been any real love in our relationship. You don't love me enough."

"What do you mean?" Heather is stunned. "Of course I love you. We're happy together."

"No, Heather. I need to find my happiness. I have to think of *my* life. I'm leaving."

"You're not happy with me?" Heather asks, her voice quivering.

"That's right. I want a more loving relationship," Mark responds.

"A more loving relationship?"

"Yes. I'm not angry with you, you know."

Life, liberty, and the pursuit of happiness. The most deeply ingrained and praiseworthy of all American values. And soul-searching. And the examined life. And not being angry. He has espoused the most widely accepted and admired values of the American people since 1776. You can't argue with that. Which is exactly what he wants.

If you disagree, you are ignorant, uncaring, critical, and uncompassionate. But you know you can't agree with what he's said because, as shocked and hurt as you are, you realize there is something not right about the combination of love, life, liberty, and the pursuit of happiness with leaving your family. There is nothing you can say. Which is exactly what he wants. But at least you know what you can *do*, now that you know these lines are just part of the Script.

JARED: We've got to talk. I can't stay with you anymore. There's no love between us.

MIMI: You can't stay with me anymore?

JARED: No, it wouldn't be honest.

MIMI: Oh, Jared, but I love you. Please don't leave me.

JARED: That's the way I thought you would react. Mimi, you're a very good person. But it wouldn't be honest.

Honesty, recognizing the good in others. What more could you ask of him? There's no arguing with these characteristics of the perfect man. And that's exactly what he wants: no argument.

If you question the values of honesty and recognition of another's worth, you seem unappreciative, argumentative, dense, uncomprehending, and amoral. But you know you can't agree with what he's said because your heart, your intuition, and your common sense tell you there is something not right about pairing honesty and the recognition of goodness with leaving your family.

He has been planning this explosive announcement for a while. In fact, he unwittingly confirms this when he says after he drops the Bomb, "That's the way I thought you would react." The planning can be particularly strenuous. For months before the vacation, Jeff Reed was working hard not only planning every detail of the trip and how he would drop the Bomb, but also strenuously reassuring Cynthia, his mistress, that he really was going to leave Amy.

Charlie had months of stressful, expensive planning, too, before the birthday party. A year previously he had decided he wasn't happy and never should have married Mindy in the first place—especially since Jackie made him feel so alive. He thought to himself that it would be wise to see a lawyer on his own, which he did—along with giving the lawyer a five-thousand-dollar retainer. That was a lot of money but Charlie felt certain that would be the last dollar he spent on lawyers. Mindy would realize right away it was a done deal and certainly wouldn't want her own lawyer. Then things might get unpleasant and she wouldn't want that.

A few months after he talked to his lawyer, Charlie decided on the elaborate birthday party where the key participant would be the process server. Charlie told him to serve Mindy with the papers just after the candles had been blown out. He said, "Just give them to her and go. It'll be easier for everyone that way." It was a brilliant idea to serve her at such a startling moment. Just the effect he wanted. No one could say a thing! It took a lot of thought, and doing it in secret wasn't easy, but it was worth all the effort.

Max had had more than a year of nerve-wracking planning. He had already bought an apartment in Chicago, which was where he rendezvoused with Beth. But getting Helena to accept that he bought the apartment as an investment had taken a lot of explaining and complicated stories, especially since he had always told Helena that downtown co-ops weren't good investments. Then he had been planning how to get his oldest son to choose the University of Illinois because a state school would be a lot cheaper than the private colleges his son had his eye on. Hard work.

It was undoubtedly just as hard, or harder, for Henry Ford II. Even though he had resources and power far beyond the average man, he also had problems the average unfaithful man wouldn't encounter. His position at the top of Ford Motor Company required numerous people to know his whereabouts every hour of the day. And wherever he was, even among strangers, he might well be recognized. What if the newspapers found out he was leaving before he was ready to drop the Bomb? Being rich and famous makes it especially difficult to operate secretly. Yessir, working in secret can be extraordinarily stressful.

Listening to other men tell how they dropped the Bomb, he has stored away the settings and language that have made other men look like heroes and will thus make him look equally good. He has been imagining how you will react and choosing strategies he thinks will minimize your anger. He includes references to as many widely admired values as he can think of so there's little you can immediately see to criticize. He lets you know he's doing this to uphold only the loftiest ideals. So, you have some catching up to do, emotionally and practically.

TIP: TAKE COMMAND.

You've been shot by a stun gun. But don't let it stun you into inaction. By taking command, you calm those around you and gather your forces. The first general you call up should be your attorney general. In other words, call a lawyer.

Get a Lawyer

Most important, get a lawyer. Women, and some men, often feel that not getting a lawyer will enable the issues to be settled in a more amicable and peaceful way. The opposite is almost always true.

First, only a lawyer can tell you what your legal rights are. Until you know that you don't know what you are, or are not, entitled to.

Second, the lawyer can handle the difficult, unpleasant, contentious part of the separation or divorce negotiations so that you don't have to. Then whatever interaction you have with your spouse can be kept on a businesslike level without emotionally depleting and unproductive arguments and accusations.

Third, even if you are thinking of mediation or arbitration or collaborative divorce, almost all mediators will advise you to see a lawyer first so that you know your legal rights. This is good advice to follow—don't go into mediation without knowing your legal rights.

There are many approaches to finding and evaluating a lawyer. You can start by asking friends who have similar circumstances, have used a family law lawyer and felt they had *good representation.*

Next you can call or locate on the Internet the offices of the State Bar for your state and ask for the names of Certified Specialists in Family Law in your county. Some states don't have a Certified Specialist designation. If that

is the case, go to the website for the American Academy
of Matrimonial Lawyers (*www.aaml.org*) for help finding a
lawyer. Members of this group must be either Certified
Specialists or have passed a proficiency exam.

Now you have some names. Don't be afraid to schedule a
first meeting with more than one lawyer. Then you can
judge if this lawyer is someone you will be comfortable
with. Look for a lawyer who wants to educate you and not
just tell you what to do. Choose a lawyer who will handle
your case as a business matter, not someone who will stir
the pot and feed your emotions.

And, if you find that you have made the wrong choice,
don't be afraid to switch lawyers.

If your financial resources are limited

We have to be honest: it can be very difficult to find a
good lawyer if you don't have the resources to pay for
one. That said, most county bar associations have some
kind of program for those with limited resources. Other
choices include contacting Legal Aid directly; contacting
the legal clinic of a law school in your area; or contacting
a nonprofit organization such as a women's group that of-
fers free or low-cost legal advice.

SCENE 2: "I LIKE LIVING ALONE"

Some men have a more gradual approach to dropping the Bomb.
It's hard to deal with the effects of nuclear war all at once—the
death and destruction, the cutting of lines of communication,

and the mushroom cloud spreading devastation beyond the immediate area. So to make it easier on themselves some men drop the Bomb in stages. The Script for the first stage goes like this:

HUSBAND: I'm moving out. I'm taking my stuff. You can reach me at my apartment.

WIFE: But you'll be there by yourself.

HUSBAND: I like living alone.

WIFE: But you always said you hate doing all the household things, the laundry and shopping and cooking. You said you were so thankful I was good at that.

HUSBAND: No, I like living alone and I like being by myself. I need some space.

WIFE: Well, that sure is different from what you said before, but I guess you know what you like.

On this spring Saturday morning Carl is outside puttering in the garage and mulling over his conversation with his friend Tim. A few weeks ago Tim told him about a mutual fishing buddy who had left his wife and gone to live with a bunch of guys who were sailor-adventurers in Mexico. It sounded like this buddy also had a girlfriend there. Just then Carl's wife, Naomi, comes outside and reminds him about the three family events they have with the kids that weekend. Carl bursts out, "This is not working. I can't live like this. I'm an adventurer, a risk-taker. I'm moving out."

"You're moving out?" Naomi doesn't hide her shock. "Are you kidding?"

"No," Carl responds. "I'm not kidding."

"But where are you going to live?" Naomi asks.

"In a cabin in the woods. I need the space to think, space away from all this."

"A cabin in the woods? Not too practical, is it? And kind of lonely."

"I like living alone."

When he says he likes living alone, you probably believe that he is speaking the truth. You think maybe he's bored with your company, tired of family obligations, weary of being around you and the kids every spare moment, and wants to be free of all this. You think he just needs to do his own thing. You're feeling very hurt to be rejected but think that from his point of view maybe what he's saying makes sense. What you must remember is that the Script lines are always chosen to make him look good. "I like living alone" is a way for him to make his exit while avoiding your anger. You really can't get angry with someone who is only expressing the most cherished ideals of American culture. Living alone, especially in a cabin in the woods, represents these ideals: rugged individualism, self-sufficiency, independence, a "can-do" attitude. You really can't argue with this. Just the result he wants. You can't argue, so there's no anger to deal with.

In truth, he can't be alone for one second. We're in Act II, Scene 2 and he's just following the Script.

Truly, he won't be alone for one single day, as we'll soon see. What's more, he's been planning for quite a while—much longer than is now apparent—to make absolutely sure he will not be alone.

Go See For Yourself

He says he likes living alone and you believe him. But
that's no reason to leave him alone. Go to his new place
to see for yourself. Visit him there. This will benefit you
in one of two ways: either you'll find out pretty quickly
that indeed he's *not* living alone, in which case you will
know how to behave; or you will be showing him that you
do take an interest in his life, you are taking him seriously, and you are willing to go to great lengths to
change the outcome of the Script.

SCENE 3: THERE'S ALWAYS SOMEONE ELSE, ALWAYS

In this scene he's continually repeating his lines from the previous
scene: he likes living alone, he needs his space, he likes being by
himself. But voices from behind the stage curtains are telling you
something very different: He isn't living alone. These voices speak
the truth in every performance of the Script because there's always someone else, *always*.

We enter Scene 3 as Lisa decides once more to get Steve to come
over and take his piles of stuff out of the garage. She's been calling him for weeks since he moved out and he has ignored her re-
quests while the mountains of clothes, sports gear, and power
tools just sit there. Lisa picks up the phone to dial Steve's new
home where he is "living alone."

LISA: Hello, who's this?

WOMAN: This is Jodi. Who's this?

LISA: What do you mean, "Who's this?" This is Lisa. Where's Steve?

JODI: Steve's here. Do you want to speak to him?

LISA: I sure do.

JODI (SHOUTING TO STEVE): Hey, Steve, Lisa's on the phone.

STEVE: Hi, Lisa. What's up?

LISA: What's up is, who's with you? That's not what I called about but who is that?

STEVE: Oh, that's Jodi from the office. We had some extra work to finish over the weekend and we thought it was easier to do it in my apartment than drive all the way to the office. I had my computer here anyway. What do you need?

LISA: I need you to come over and get your stuff out of the garage. But I also need you to tell me what that woman's doing in your apartment. I thought you liked being alone.

STEVE: I do like being alone and I just told you what we're doing. We had some work to finish.

LISA: Okay, well please come over later and get your stuff.

STEVE: Yeah, when I can.

WIFE: (on the phone) You sure have your machine on a lot in the evening. Can't you answer the phone?

HUSBAND: Well, I work on my computer and I just have to concentrate. I can't be interrupted by the phone.

WIFE: You always used to pick up the phone even when you were working on the computer. It's not that there's someone there with you, is it?

HUSBAND: Are you kidding? I'm so busy with stuff I have no time for that. I'm just here alone and I like it.

Even close friends and relatives may believe him when he says he likes living alone, just needs some space, some time to think. They may believe him when he says there's no other woman. But in all the stories we have heard, in all the discussions we have had with experts, we know that regardless of what anyone else thinks, THERE'S ALWAYS SOMEONE ELSE. *ALWAYS*. These lines are never spoken on stage. But they are part of the Script in every scene from the middle of Act I going forward.

Women tend to think it's the men who are the strong ones, who can handle anything on their own. But they can't be alone for a second. In fact, until he has someone lined up, he won't leave because he absolutely can't be alone. Having "the other woman" who is committed to him gives him the courage to leave.

No matter what he says—"I like living alone," "I need some space," "I need time to think"—no matter how sure friends and outsiders are that in *this* case it's really true and there is no other woman, there's always someone else, always.

TIP: GO BACK TO CHILDHOOD GAMES.

This will be repeatedly useful. Here we recommend recalling and then calling out "LIAR, LIAR, PANTS ON FIRE."

It's gut-wrenching to confront the hard facts in front of you—someone you trusted completely, maybe for many

years, is not telling the truth. He is . . . He is a . . . He is a
li . . . He is a LIAR!

The simple childhood refrain, rearranged slightly, will
help you to keep that in mind. His pants are on fire or, in
other words, there *is* someone else and he has lied to
cover it up.

Pants on fire, liar, liar.

No Hope

There may be a point where the pain has grown beyond
hope of relief and it has sliced through love, trust, and
caring beyond repair.

If this point comes don't resist the conclusion that there
is no hope of reconciliation. Continuing to hope when
there is no chance of reconciliation may inhibit you from
protecting and preparing yourself for the future. Such
things as getting a lawyer and thinking about finances
and living arrangements can be very important now. See
Act II, Scene 5, "I'm Going to Take Care of You," to understand how things can turn out quite differently from
the way it now appears they will.

SCENE 4: "YOU'LL BE BETTER OFF WITHOUT ME"

SUSIE: I wish you would change your mind. I wish you would come
back. I wish you would tell me why you left.

NED: I'm doing this for you.

SUSIE: For me? I want you to come back. I don't want you to leave.

NED: You'll be better off without me.

Susie is absolutely stunned. After telling her how courageous, wise, caring, moral, appealing, discerning, admired, and generous he is, and how difficult, dense, dowdy, and crazy *she* is, shouldn't he think there could be nothing better than to be still married to him? Why would Ned say "You'll be better off without me?"

DEANNA: Would you go for counseling with me? We have so much together. I think we could work things out with some help. I know you said you liked living alone but it always seemed to me that you liked being with me and the family.

GREG: Yes, I do like being with the family, but this doesn't need to change that. It'll all be the same. We'll still have the family we've always had.

DEANNA: But I want us all to be together.

GREG: It wouldn't be fair to you to keep you married to someone who doesn't love you.

Deanna wants to say something because she so much wants Greg to come back but she doesn't know what to say. She feels crushingly hurt all over again when Greg says he doesn't love her. At the same time, she feels Greg has her best interests at heart if he's willing to make such a personal sacrifice because he cares so much about what is good for her. She hadn't realized he was putting her best interests above his own, that he was moving out into the unknown so that she could be truly happy. He must really be a good person.

Greg gives himself a pat on the back. "Boy, I can do this." He has listened very carefully over the years to what other men have said after they dropped the Bomb. He has just now seen the true value of this passed down wisdom: Deanna is speechless with appreciation of his consideration of her. He's shown her the deep love of personal sacrifice. It's a greater, deeper love than just sex or a dozen roses or diamond earrings. It's the greatest love of all—incredible personal sacrifice for the good of another human being. The best thing is, Deanna and the world admire his nobility but in reality it is no sacrifice at all. What he hasn't told Deanna is that he has been seeing Cheryl for six months now. The truth is he is doing exactly what he wants. He *can* have everything.

Charlie and Scott have wrapped towels around their necks after a vigorous game of tennis on a sweltering day.

"So you goin' home now, Charlie?" Scott asks.

"Well, my new home, yes," Charlie replies. "I don't know if I mentioned it last time we played but I finally decided to separate from Gwen. She never would have been happy with me anyway."

Scott thinks about this and is impressed. "Charlie left Gwen and likely has some young blonde he's seeing. But at the same time, he's not leaving people with the feeling that he abandoned his wife. He's letting people know that even if he had stayed, his wife still wouldn't have been happy. Gwen must be a real complainer. The kind of person that no matter how much you do, it's still not right. But even with all this, Charlie's telling us he put his wife's happiness first. *And* he's got the blonde. Sounds exciting. I gotta remember how Charlie handled this. The way he's done it, he's coming out looking pretty good."

Scott is learning the Script.

SUSAN: Cal, would you tell me what it is about me that you don't like? What did I do wrong?

CAL: I'm not going to tell you.

SUSAN: I want to know so that in case I get married again I don't make the same mistake, whatever it was.

CAL: If you're about to get married, then I'll tell you.

SUSAN: I would like to know now.

CAL: I can't tell you. But I do know I couldn't in good conscience submit you and the kids to the vagaries of my changing personality.

Susan steps back to think for a minute. She was sure that she had done something terribly wrong, maybe many things terribly wrong, during the marriage and that's why Cal decided to leave. But now he appears to be saying that it is something going on in *his* personality that caused him to leave. "Gosh," Susan thinks, "he has something going on so serious that he couldn't even talk to me about it. I guess he didn't want to burden me. And now he cares so much about the kids and my welfare that he is actually taking this enormous step just for us. Yes, he does have a conscience. I never thought of it that way. But Cal would never say something so deeply moral and spiritual if it wasn't true. He's doing this to help us."

It may seem that way, but he's just following the Script.

He's done a great job getting you to think he's left only because he's putting your interests first and he wants to help you. The Script has told him that he'll feel a little less guilty and come out looking very noble if he says he left to improve your situation. But we can predict he is not planning to improve it with too much money.

TIP: DON'T FALL FOR IT.

He's not putting your interests first. He's been thinking of himself all along. He wants to have his cake and eat it too. He wants to be able to do the thing society thinks is wrong—leave his wife and children—and he wants to be thought of as noble while he does it.

Here is your own answer for when he says he's doing it for you: "It's kind of you to consider me at this late juncture, but I don't believe a word you say."

SCENE 5: "I'M GOING TO TAKE CARE OF YOU"

Eddie moved out of the family home just a few days ago. But he has come back to talk to Anita and is sitting down with her in the family room. He says very earnestly to her, "I want to be your best friend. I'm going to take care of you. You needn't have any concerns."

Anita is so relieved to hear this. All kinds of worries had been swirling through her head. Now her mind is at rest. She sees that Eddie will take care of all of her needs and she won't have to worry about anything. She assumes she'll get half of everything and continue to be able to live the way she has.

However, Eddie means something quite different. He means "I'm going to take care of you on my terms. I'm going to decide how much you need to live on."

MIKE: You're making yourself crazy with worry.

FRANCINE: Well, I *am* worried.

MIKE: Don't worry. Everything will be okay. I'm going to take care of you.

Mike sounds very reassuring and Francine seems much better after hearing him say everything will be okay. But again his real intent is very different—he wants Francine to feel so comfortable that she lets her guard down and looks the other way. Then Mike can proceed to "take care" of her on his own terms—retaining the bulk of their assets for himself.

Mike really believes he's being fair. He worked hard to get where he is in his career. His talents and skills and all the late nights in the office made the life they led possible. He deserves to walk away with the lion's share. Later on Mike will learn that Francine looks at it differently. She feels that while Mike has worked hard and is very good at what he does, he never would have achieved what he did without her as a partner.

MATT: There you go exaggerating everything. What is the *problem*?

NICOLE: I just don't feel secure about my future. Or the kids' future. You have a good job. I can't live on what I make from my part-time work. I don't feel sure that you're going to help me have what I need to live on.

MATT: You're getting upset about nothing.

NICOLE: But it's not nothing. Will you help me?

MATT: Can you see me letting you down?

Nicole thinks, "Well, I never thought you would let me down. But you just did because you left me and the kids. So now I don't know. You sound so sincere. I guess you wouldn't let me down. I guess you will help me."

Matt has just spent two hours making a list of all his and Nicole's possessions—the house, the cars, his motorcycle, the Jet Ski, the furniture, his sports memorabilia collection, the antique glass-ware Nicole collects, and some jewelry he's given Nicole. Then he starts a list of the financial assets—the checking account, some money they've saved in a joint brokerage account, and the college savings plans they have for the kids. Matt thinks about the money in his pension plan at work, an IRA he's contributed to for ten years (and he just arranged for the statement to come to his office instead of the house), the bonus pool that's sure to get him at least $10,000 at the end of the year, and the investment he made with three other men in a golf equipment business that's turned out quite well. He says to himself, "No need to put these on the list; they're mine. And even if they aren't, Nicole won't realize that anyway." After he's finished he picks up the phone and calls Nicole to say, "I'm coming over in half an hour. Let's sit down and go over some things. We can just make a list and get everything divided up between ourselves in no time."

Nicole is surprised at this call because she hadn't even been thinking about dividing their property. It was only two weeks ago that Matt had shocked her by saying that he was having an identity crisis that required him to have some space, alone. She isn't prepared to go over their things. She has no list. But she is missing Matt and needs some help with things around the house so she says, "Okay, sure, come on over."

Half an hour later she hears the garage door going up and a car pulling in. A minute later Matt opens the door and walks in.

"Hi, Matt," Nicole says.

"Hi," Matt says. "You look good. Everything all right?"

"Yeah, sure," Nicole answers, not really sure at all.

"Okay. I have a list of everything we have. Let's sit down and get this all worked out. No need to make something simple into something complicated."

"Sure, Matt, we can work this out between us. I want everything to be peaceful."

"Look at this list. It's everything. Of course, we can each keep our own cars. If you need a new one next year, just call me. I'll help you find one. You wouldn't want the motorcycle or the Jet Ski or my sports collection, so I'll take those. I don't think the entertainment center means that much to you so I'll take that. Okay?"

"Yes, it seems okay," Nicole says.

In fact, Nicole's mind is on a dozen other things—who's going to pick up the kids from ice skating in half an hour, when will she get a chance to bake for her women's church group meeting tomorrow night, how early will she be able to reach the doctor tomorrow morning to ask about Robbie's earache, how will she pay the huge plumber's bill for the sink that got stopped up, and how will she manage without a man in the house.

"Good. So then there's the checking account and the brokerage account and we can just split those in half. And of course the kids' college savings account which, you know, those accounts are gonna grow about 20% a year and that'll be more than enough to take care of their tuition by the time they're ready for college."

Nicole says "Okay," but even in her state of shock from Matt's sudden leaving, she realizes that she really has no idea if it's okay. But she doesn't want to ask too many questions or dispute in any way what Matt is saying because she doesn't want to make him angry or upset. Nor does she want to say that she would like some time to think about it all, because then Matt would think

she didn't trust him or that she doubted his abilities to divide things properly. So Nicole nods her head yes to reaffirm her okay. She really hopes this is all a nightmare and she will wake up tomorrow morning and Matt will be in bed beside her.

Then Matt goes on, "We'll sell the house. You and the kids can get an apartment in the Valleyview complex."

Nicole starts to look anxious. She has so much to do and all this complicated talk is making her nervous. She gets up and starts moving things aimlessly around the kitchen. Matt can see that this is completely unlike Nicole's usual organized self and her agitation makes him feel like he has to work even harder to have things his way. So he says, "Nicole, sit down. Relax. I want you to have enough money. We'll see how much money you need to live on and I'll give that to you."

Matt quickly backtracked because he realized he went too far. He wanted to act conciliatory to get her to think he was being fair. The Script has taught him to get her comfortable so that the last thing she'll be thinking of is dollars and cents.

One week later Nicole is talking to Matt on the phone.

NICOLE: I've thought about it and I want to get my own lawyer. I talked to a couple of my friends and they told me that's what I should do.

MATT: Look, that's completely unnecessary. Let's not give all the money to the lawyers. I'll come over and we'll just sit down and divide things up. No reason we can't be civil about this. My lawyer will get it all written up.

NICOLE: Well, my friend Jill gave me the name of a lawyer to call and I'm going to call her.

MATT: What kind of vindictive women are telling you to get a lawyer? Don't you know that all lawyers want is the money? We're not going to give all our money to lawyers. The lawyers will eat up my whole bonus from last year at the rate you're going. If we just cooperate with each other it will work out better for both of us. Let's just sit down.

After hearing what Matt is saying, Nicole is not sure what to do. She is weighing in her mind the conflicting advice, all from people she has always trusted. Several friends have told her she should have her own lawyer. "But now Matt is saying that these friends are just vindictive women. Maybe they are. Matt always was such a good judge of character. But why would my friends give me bad advice?" she thinks. Then again, she thinks about lawyers she has heard of who have run up enormous bills. If that happened to her, she and Matt would have less for themselves. "Matt is right," she concludes, "it'll work out better if we just sit down."

"Let's sit down" is a leitmotif in the Script the men follow. Let's sit down and talk about dividing the money. Let's sit down and divide the property. Let's sit down and talk. Let's sit down and just be friends. The unspoken Script says that if you don't agree to sitting down you're not cooperative, not friendly, not nice, not decent, don't know how reasonable people do business. "Why won't you sit down?" He's really saying this in order to force you to answer in a way and with words that make you into the crazy, unreasonable, demanding, uncivil one—traits you probably don't have and don't want to be known for having. He

thinks if you sit down he will be in control. Sitting down also makes him feel comfortable, at ease, makes him feel like you'll go along with what he's done, that he can have his cake and eat it too.

So either you "sit down" and probably come out the worse for it financially and emotionally, or you don't sit down and he tells people you're unreasonable, uncooperative, demanding, and crazy. It seems like a no-win situation.

TIP: DON'T SIT DOWN.

Don't sit down. In fact, do the opposite, stand up for yourself. Sitting down means being relaxed, comfortable, not being on high alert.

As much as he says he's going to take care of you and as hard as it is to believe that he isn't going to take care of you, the truth is: He's *not* going to take care of you. You must be on high alert, *now*. Someone you trusted has shown himself not to be trustworthy. We can predict that the infidelity which started in Act I is virtually certain to continue as he works to protect his sticks and bricks.

Not only do you have to be standing up for yourself, you have to be ready to hear, and to ignore, the critical comments your husband will predictably make behind your back. "She's out of control." "She's being influenced by her spiteful friends and a bunch of greedy lawyers." "Anybody with an ounce of dignity would just keep this between ourselves. But, no, she has to be vindictive." "If she really had the good of the family at heart, she'd just sit down. You can see how selfish she is."

Six months later Matt calls Nicole after getting a call from his lawyer about a proposal on how their assets will be split.

"Nicole, you are the most difficult, vengeful woman alive. Where do you get off thinking you're entitled to all this money?"

"Matt, this is what my lawyer told me is my rightful share. And the way I understand it, your lawyer, after going over everything, has agreed," Nicole says.

"All you want is my money," Matt shouts into the phone. "That's all you've ever wanted."

Nicole feels wounded by this remark because she never felt that way about her marriage to Matt. She does think for a second that, of course, she enjoyed the things that money could buy, and was always happy that Matt made a nice income. Nicole is hurt and insulted that, after Matt told her that she and the kids could live in the plain and ordinary Valleyview Apartments, she found out that he and the other woman were moving into a large custom-designed home in a new subdivision. She thinks, "Shouldn't I be able to live at the same level that he does?" She feels that Matt is telling her that she is worth less than he is, that she is not as good as he is. Because Matt said it, though, and because she's used to believing him, she wonders briefly if he's right that she was more interested in his money than in him. But she realizes that if he paints her as the bad guy then he is the good guy. She concludes that the assets that will be hers are rightfully hers.

The Biggest Antitrust Case
in the World

It's the biggest antitrust case in the world. The institution of marriage itself is based on trust starting with the marriage vows, each one giving his and her word to the other. He has broken that trust but it's hard to believe that someone you loved, respected, and admired would do this. When you act to protect yourself, when you ask questions, when you operate on high alert, when you operate in opposition instead of in partnership, you feel you are saying "I don't trust you," and that this means that *you* are breaking your vow of trust. "Is it just me," you may wonder, "or does every woman feel this way?"

Every woman feels this way.

Know that you're not breaking any vow of trust. You are simply protecting yourself and your children from someone who has shown he cannot be trusted and who, we can predict, is not acting in your interests now.

The Good Girl

You may still be hoping that if you're good enough, he'll come back. Women are trained from girlhood to be "good." It is natural to think that if you're nice, coopera-tive, sweet, conciliatory, and do what he says, he will find you much more appealing than if you act like you don't trust him, do things that he calls "vindictive," assert your rights, and get your own lawyer. You think you will be so appealing in your gentleness that he'll realize very soon that he made a terrible mistake.

It almost never happens that way. Unfortunately, what often does happen is that if you don't stand up for yourself, you and your children will come out worse. When he is in this fantasy state, you will *never* be good enough.

SCENE 6: "HE WOULD NEVER DO THAT"

"Hi, Louisa, it's Susie. I'm calling to make sure you can come to the fundraising meeting tonight for the children's park."

"Yes, Susie, I'll be there," Louisa says.

"I wasn't sure," Susie says, "because I heard from Hedy that Bill is telling everybody you're not doing well since he left. He says that you're all over the place, completely spacey, and impossible to deal with."

"Bill is saying that? I doubt it. Hedy is making that up. He would never say that. He's not that kind of person."

.   .   .

He's going to try to make you look like you're angry all the time, selfish, greedy, difficult, flaky, and downright crazy. He's going to criticize you to your children, your friends, and, of course, to *his* colleagues and his friends.

Cindy and Donna were walking around a lake near their homes in St. Paul early one morning. Cindy couldn't believe what was happening to her. Her husband had just walked out after twenty-three years of marriage. Donna knew Cindy needed a friend to talk to, so they had taken this walk around the lake several times over the last few weeks. Donna's husband had left her years before so she knew how devastated Cindy must feel at this point. Donna also knew, from her own experience and from talking to friends, that right now Cindy had to keep an eye on her assets because her husband had probably already hidden money and he was sure to be hiding more.

A couple of days later Donna said to Cindy, "Cindy, watch out, Ken's sure to start to hide money."

Cindy's immediate response was "He'd never do that. Not Ken. He wouldn't hide money from me." Donna knew it was very likely to happen but she said nothing because Cindy was already so upset.

The next week Donna got a call from Cindy that confirmed her prediction. "Hi, Donna. It's Cindy. You'll never believe this but I just opened our savings account statement and ten thousand dollars is gone from the account. How did you *know?*"

. . .

We're in Act II, Scene 6. You may be saying to yourself, "This won't happen to me. My husband is different. He's not that kind of person." You know him as a man with values, standards by which he lives, a man who would never do anything opposite to the values he's always stated. You even remember times when he told you "I would never do that." He may have been very critical of how President Clinton behaved in the Lewinsky scandal. He was always sympathetic to women whose husbands had been unfaithful and left them. You think he's different. But he's not different.

Even though he has moved out, you still trust him. You have always known him as a man who would never hide money from you, never turn his attention away from the children, or try to take things from you.

No woman wants to believe her husband is following the Script. It makes her feel foolish, naive, and ignorant for having believed what he was saying. "Is it just me," you may wonder over and over, "or does every woman feel this way?" It's not just you; every woman feels this way.

Veronica and Myra have just sat down for dinner in a restaurant near their homes. Veronica is so happy to have a night out because since Dan left she has hardly had a minute to herself. They order their meals and after the waiter walks away Myra says, "I happened to run into Dan the other day and he said some things about you that got me worried about how you're doing. He said you act like you're in outer space with the kids and it must be because you don't feel good about yourself."

Veronica had been feeling very good about herself for having kept everything going in spite of the shock of Dan's leaving. So she is astounded to hear what Myra has said. She feels sure Myra must have misunderstood Dan, because he would never say something so untruthful about her. So she says to Myra, "Dan would never say that about me. He knows I'm doing amazingly well."

Cori has made an appointment with her financial adviser because now that Mel has left she feels she has to pay attention to her assets and future needs. She comes into Kalmann Investments and is shown into Mary Kalmann's office. Cori begins by asking Mary about how she and Mel will pay for college for their two children, who are now fifteen and seventeen years old. Cori says to Mary, "I think it will be fine. Mel has always said he wants the children to have the best education possible. Besides what we've saved and the kids' summer jobs, Mel has plenty of money to send them wherever they want to go."

Mary waits for a second and then says, "Cori, I have to tell you that in my twenty years in the investment business I have never seen a divorced father pay for college after a child turns eighteen."

Cori immediately responds, "Oh, that might be so but Mel is different. He's not that kind of person."

Mary doesn't want to argue with Cori so she says nothing, but she can predict with near 100% accuracy that, unless a court has ordered otherwise, Mel will contribute nothing for college for his children after they reach eighteen.

It's hard to accept but it's true. You think He Would Never Do That . . . but he will do *just that*! He's following the Script.

"Mom, Dad says if we live at home for college, you're going to run our lives. He says you'll tell us what courses to take, what sports to go out for, how to study, who to date, what to wear, what to eat," seventeen-year-old Ryan says.

Ryan, have I ever acted that way to you and Jessica? I can see you can make mature decisions and I hardly ever tell you what to do."

"Well, Mom, that's what Dad told Grandma," Ryan says.

"Ryan, Grandma's getting older. She may not remember what Dad said. Dad's not that kind of person," Dana responds with as much confidence as she can muster.

TIP: BUY SALT.

Buy salt. Lots of it. You'll need it—because you should be taking his every statement with a grain of salt. Undoubtedly, starting even before you were married, you trusted him and continued to trust him. While you may look back and think, "Was I crazy or just plain stupid or naive to trust him?" you weren't and aren't crazy, stupid, or naive.

Our whole society is based on trust—the use of checks and credit cards; any contract with someone to do something, whether a plumber or an employer; friendship; social relationships. Any written or verbal contract is based on trust—the other party will do what they said or signed they would do. Checks rely on trust because if it wasn't for the overwhelming number of people who back up their checks with money, we couldn't use checks. If we bring in a car for repair, we trust that the car mechanic will fix it as he says and he trusts us to pay. If we make a date with a friend, each is trusting that the other will show up. If we buy shares of stock in a company, we trust the executives and employees will do an honest job of running the company. The same goes for marriage—it is a written and verbal contract to live by the marriage vows. Each spouse trusts the other to do just that.

Even though he has shown signs of untrustworthiness, you still want to trust him—you've always done so and it's very hard to change. It's very difficult to live with someone, whether it's a spouse, an employer, or someone else, whose every word and deed you have to doubt. Life becomes very difficult when someone you need to trust—a spouse, an employer, an employee—has violated that trust. You still need to "do business" with that person, but how?

Throw some salt around: Stop trusting so much. Because we can predict that much of what he's telling you will turn out not to be true. "I'm going to take care of you." "I'm laying everything on the table with the money." "We can settle this fairly for both of us without all those high-priced lawyers."

If you act on the basis of trusting everything he says, you will probably come out on the short end.

SCENE 7: "THE LAST TO KNOW"

Heddy and Gabrielle have finished their workout at the gym and decide to take another twenty minutes to have a quick lunch and catch up. They have just taken the first bite of their salads when Gabrielle starts talking excitedly, launching into a story she obviously can't wait to tell—the latest news she's heard about their mutual friend Christina and her husband, Paul.

"Did you hear that Paul's been seen around with another woman?" Gabrielle asks.

"Really?" Heddy says, "that's disgraceful. But why would he do that? Christina is gorgeous. We're both here at the gym trying to slim down to look just like her."

"I don't know," Gabrielle says, "but I'm not going to be the one to tell her. Are you going to tell her?"

"Heavens no," Heddy says. "We're best friends but I'm not going to get mixed up in that. Who knows. It may not even be true. I can't see Paul doing that. He's got a big-time job. They've got three kids, a house they just spent a fortune fixing up. I don't get why he'd risk losing all that. I'm staying out of it."

Six months after Heddy and Gabrielle have their conversation, Christina is sitting at the computer in the family room facing a chore she hates—bill paying. She comes to the cell phone bills and sees that there are two different bills in Paul's name this month and both bills seem kind of high. Christina decides that she better look at each call and compare the new bills to previous bills so she can understand what's causing such big charges.

As Christina is looking at the last few months' bills, she tries to figure out who each call is to. She recognizes the numbers of different offices in Paul's company; she recognizes his mother's number. But there are also quite a few calls each month to a number she doesn't recognize. It's a local number, just in the next town; she can tell by the exchange. Christina decides she'd better try the number and see whose it is before she calls TowerCell to say there's a mistake on the bill.

Christina dials. A recording comes on. "Hi, this is Jen. Please leave a message. I want to hear from you." Christina has no idea who

Jen is and decides to wait until the evening when someone is likely to pick up. She tries that evening. Still a machine. She waits until the next evening to try again, wondering who Jen could possibly be and why Paul would be calling a woman's home at all times of the day and night. She starts to get anxious. She thinks to herself, "This isn't someone Paul 'shouldn't' be calling, is it? I'm sure it isn't." When she tries again at dinnertime the next evening, a woman answers. "Hello, hello. Hello? Paul, is that you?"

Christina has forgotten Jen might have caller ID. She hangs up silently. She knows that having a woman answer like that is kind of suspicious, but she's sure Paul will have a very sensible business reason why he has made calls to her. She decides she'll just ask Paul directly when he comes home. When she hears him coming in half an hour later, Christina is so anxious that, as soon as Paul walks in the door, she asks him, "Do you know someone named Jen?"

Paul says, "What do you mean?"

Christina says, "Well, it seems you know someone by that name. Who is she?"

Paul says, "A woman I know."

Christina says, "What do you mean 'know'?"

Paul says, "I don't invade your privacy, do I? Please don't invade mine."

Christina's anxiety is not quelled but she doesn't want to get into an argument with Paul just now, and she's still hanging onto hope that there is a good explanation. Maybe Jen is a potential big new customer for Paul's company and he doesn't want to jinx the deal by talking about her, Christina thinks.

. . .

Harriet and Josie are taking their coffee break at EnterpriseSolutions when Harriet says, "Paul is sure keeping some odd office hours lately. What's going on? Is he still trying to land that big account?"

Josie answers, "No, I know what it is. He has another woman."

Harriet says, "What do you mean?"

Josie says, "Well, I just figured it out. I was starting to notice a while back that he would close his door a lot to make calls. I thought it was that big account that was so confidential. Then over the last few months he had me send flowers a few times to a woman, not Christina. Then recently I took some strange messages, very secretive sounding, from Terrasse Jewelers. Then just last week when I was here working late and Paul did have his door open, I heard him saying on the phone, 'Jen, baby, I can't talk now. I'll call you later. Wait up for me. Bye, baby.' Then I knew."

Harriet says, "What should we do when Christina calls the office? Should we say something?"

Josie answers, "Are you kidding? I don't want to lose my job. Don't say a word."

Christina decides a gym break is what she needs. Paul left her devastated three months ago when he moved out of their home to live alone, saying he needed his space. But because since then Paul's words have expressed caring and trustworthiness she has felt somewhat reassured.

As Christina walks into the gym she runs into Gabrielle. "Hi, Gabrielle," Christina says. Gabrielle's face immediately takes on a sorrowful look.

"Oh, my dear Christina," Gabrielle says, "how are you, honey? Let's skip working out and sit down to talk. I know you must be having a rough time. What are dear friends for, if not to support you and help you at a time like this?"

"Okay," Christina says. "That would be nice."

"So what is Paul doing now?" Gabrielle asks. "Still running around with that woman?"

"Woman, what do you mean, 'woman'?" Christina is almost too shocked to speak.

"Honey," Gabrielle says, "you didn't know? How can you be so naive?"

"Please don't call me naive, and tell me what you mean," Christina says anxiously.

"Honey, Heddy and I have known for ages that Paul was fooling around. You don't mean you trusted him, do you?"

"Yes, I did trust him, Gabrielle. And until this moment I trusted you, but now I see that I can't. Why didn't you tell me?"

"Well, if you were too blind to see it on your own, then my telling you wouldn't have done any good," Gabrielle shoots back defensively.

Christina gets up, says good-bye, and tells Gabrielle that she thinks she'd better be off now to take care of some errands before the kids come home from school. In fact, Christina goes to her car and just sits there alone, feeling so hurt that Gabrielle and Heddy knew what Paul was doing and didn't say a thing. She thinks, "Paul betrayed me, now I see that Gabrielle and Heddy betrayed me. Do I have any friends?"

Christina realizes that the quickest way to get Paul to straighten out the car insurance mess that's just developed is to call him at his office. She dials and Josie answers. "Hi, Christina," Josie says, "how can I help you?"

"Could you tell Paul to call the insurance company and get this policy mess straightened out?"

"I'll tell him. Christina, I knew these kinds of messes would happen. It's always that way when the men leave all of a sudden. Well, it really wasn't all of a sudden. I guess it was all of a sudden to you. But here around the office we've known for a while."

"Known for a while? Are you serious?" Christina thinks for a moment then says, "Now I know why Harriet and you were so cold to me sometimes. I wish you had told me the truth."

"I'll give Paul your message. Anything else?" Josie asks.

"No," Christina answers and hangs up.

She feels in turmoil once again. She thinks, "They've been talking behind my back all this time, picking apart my marriage, probably saying I was a terrible wife, saying other awful things about me. I was betrayed again."

"Is it just me," you may wonder, "or does every woman feel this way?" *Every woman feels this way.*

The wife is sometimes the last to know. It's another stab in the heart because not only has he left but there were other people who knew for quite a while, dissected and criticized you behind your back, and betrayed you with their silence.

It's not entirely surprising when the wife is the last to know. An unfaithful man often lets his guard down more among other people than his wife. He may even brag about his exploits to his close men friends.

TIP: YOU DONE RIGHT.

You will have people telling you that you did wrong. They will use this logic—you trusted him.

He did you wrong.

That proves you shouldn't have trusted him.

Therefore you did wrong.

Tell them they are wrong and this is why:

It is your devotion to your marriage and your husband, and your faith in the institution of marriage, that allowed you to live in peace without suspicion or constant vigilance of your partner.

You are not foolish, gullible, naive, unconscious of your surroundings, or a victim. You were sticking to your values. Give yourself credit.

SCENE 8: "I'M NOT SLEEPING WITH HER"
OR
"WE'RE NOT HAVING SEX"

Some women suspect that their husbands are sleeping with someone before they leave. Other women don't find out until long after the Bomb has been dropped. In either case, the feelings are the same.

Gordon comes home late and tired from work. It's one time too many for Celia and, after thinking back over some strange and inexplicable things that have happened over the past few months—questions she asked him that had convoluted and suspicious answers, and a woman's name that had cropped up on a slip of paper and some phone calls to the house—Celia confronts Gordon with questions and then an accusation.

CELIA: Where were you?

GORDON: Stop asking so many questions.

CELIA: You're a married man. How could you? You're sleeping with her.

GORDON: That's not true.

CELIA: You know you're sleeping with her.

GORDON: I told you. I'm not sleeping with her.

You don't know what to believe. Your instinct tells you they're having sex. You can just feel that they're undressed together, touching, kissing, and arousing each other. At the least they're talking to each other with intimate, sex-filled language . . . and he's excited in the same way he would be if he were . . . well, having sex with her. But you're being told the opposite by someone you have always trusted and want to trust. You feel *you* must be wrong, *you* must be crazy, *you* must be lacking in understanding, *you* must be the one drawing faulty conclusions.

MEAGAN: Hi, Rita? It's Meagan.

"Ooo, Daniel, yes," Jolie says as the sex talk envelops the two of them. They are as intense as if they were plotting a murder—and they are. The murder of a soul.

They continue the stimulating conversation and then Daniel gets up quickly as he realizes it's time for him to head for home before his wife gets angry that he's late for dinner and starts to question him about why. Daniel walks to his car thinking that a whole evening in bed with Gabby doesn't come close to the excited, alive feeling he gets from just talking to Jolie for an hour.

And he can honestly say he's not sleeping with her. Isn't that what the dictionary that Ted and Brian gave him says?

This dictionary has been handed around to a lot of people. Even well-known politicians use it. For example, Newt Gingrich's infidelities have been well-documented. What's interesting is that even these politicians carefully consult the same dictionary as Ted and Brian and Daniel and Gordon. We know this because one of Gingrich's mistresses is quoted as saying, "We had oral sex. He prefers that modus operandi because then he can say, 'I never slept with her.' "

"I did not have sexual relations with that woman, Miss Lewinsky."

President Clinton made this statement to the American people. Many Americans had an uneasy feeling about what he said. People felt that it was not the whole truth as we knew the meaning of these words. But people also wanted to trust, and had been taught to trust, what the highest official in the land was telling them. When the president takes the oath of office he pledges to uphold the Constitution and the laws of the land. In America, this includes telling the truth. This is every president's vow to the American people. So we tried to put aside our doubts and the uneasy feeling we had about this oddly phrased statement.

Later, when we found out that in his grand jury testimony he said that the meaning of "having sex" depends on what your definition of "is" is, we were even more confused.

However, many Americans came back to the fact that we knew in our hearts he was being unfaithful to his wife. We knew he was doing things with Monica that involved sexual feelings, arousal, and orgasm that a married man doesn't do with someone other than his wife, at least according to most Americans' morality.

The American public felt like the betrayed wife. The president made statements that we couldn't understand and then made us feel as if *we* were falsely accusing him, *we* didn't know the truth, *we* didn't understand English, *we* were crazy.

As if *we* didn't know it depends on what the definition of "is" is, or the definition of sexual relations.

We want you to know that you're not wrong, you're not crazy, you're not lacking in understanding! He's pulled the Dictionary Switching Game!

TIP: BUY "THE ABRIDGED ADULTERER'S DICTIONARY."

This is the dictionary he slipped in behind the plain brown wrapper in Act I, Scene 8 ("This Isn't Fair") when you were facing stage right. Once you've read the AAD you'll know what definitions he's going by.

The definition for "having sex, sleeping with her" is "penetration of a vagina by a penis," henceforth known as "is is" sex. There are no additional definitions even for Old English or modern slang. That's it. Very clear. Very concise.

All of the rest of the English-speaking world goes by the Unabridged "You Know It When You Feel It" Dictionary.* **Definitions in this dictionary often follow Supreme Court Justice Potter Stewart's definition of hard-core pornography: "I know it when I see it." You know it. They're having sex. He's sleeping with her. And you're not crazy. He wants to make you think you're crazy, but it's just part of the Script.**

The two highest courts, the Supremes on earth and the Supreme in heaven, have ruled—you're not crazy, your understanding of the English language is perfect, and his appeal won't work. They're having sex.

SCENE 9: THE COURAGEOUS CHEATER

The Courageous Cheater, our man, a hero, the stuff of legend and myth, has been the main character in the fable passed verbally man to man for generations as a true legend always is. The story is sometimes enhanced to emphasize his incredible bravery— imagine him slaying the dragon of unhappiness along with the wife, whom he believes to be the dragon's accomplice. Then, of course, capturing the ravenhaired maiden.

It always appeared that each man started on the path to heroism as a lone adventurer, creating the legend piece by piece through his own individual genius and invention. He made himself look

---

*Definition for "Having Sex" from the Unabridged "You Know It When You Feel It" Dictionary: Having Sex: active verb, alt. interactive noun—Penetration of the vagina by a penis, or any sexual activity such as oral sex, manual sex, aural sex, "that certain look" sex, "sweet nothings" sex, dancing sex.

like a trailblazer, overcoming great obstacles with each move forward, enhancing his character with every step. He presented himself as the only man ever to have achieved such heights of bravery.

But with the Script now in print women everywhere know differently. He is no more than a good rote learner, with even the best actors among unfaithful men adding a personal touch only occasionally.

He's learned, though, it's always best if courage doesn't look too easy. He's not much of a hero if he didn't climb the highest mountains to get there. So the road to being the courageous cheater starts with manufactured complexity.

CAROL: Please, James, tell me what it is. Why do you want to leave me and the children? I want to understand. Maybe we can do something about it, whatever it is. I just don't understand why.

JAMES: It's complicated. Way too complicated to do anything about. And way too late now.

CAROL: Please, James, try to explain why you don't love me anymore. I'll understand what you're saying. Even if I can only grasp some of it, I just want to know why.

JAMES: There's no purpose served in going into the details. Only God knows the real truth of matters like this. This is not something I did lightly.

CAROL: I didn't say you did it lightly. I just want to understand better why you don't love me anymore.

JAMES: It's very complex.

Even Hollywood stars like Ethan Hawke go deep into manufactured complexity. In responding to questions about whether infidelity led to his separation from his wife of five years, Uma Thurman, and their two children, he is quoted as saying, "The story of us breaking up over infidelity has been an annoying one. If our problems were that simple, we'd still be together." It's very complicated, right?

You are completely baffled. You can't see the complexity he claims is there. You start to think that maybe your ability to understand something like this is limited, that you are unable to grasp deep meaning the way he apparently can. His mind sees layer upon layer of complex, profound truths, too deep to put into words, it appears. No ordinary mortal could understand this profundity. Only God and our man can plumb these depths, it seems.

It is only natural to believe what he is telling you. If he says it's very complicated, it seems it must be so. If you can't see how complex it is, then that proves that even if he put it into words, you wouldn't understand it.

You are just like the wise child who can't see the Emperor's new clothes— because there aren't any.

You will feel less confused and hurt if you know this claim to complexity is part of the Script. He is intentionally portraying leaving you and the children as something that is at once courageous and complex, when it is in fact neither one. Your faulty and broken heart will be no match for his Purple Heart. The Script has taught him that your mind will also be no match for God and deep spiritual meaning. Include these divine references, the Script has taught him.

. . .

"I'm a risk taker. It's very courageous to step away and start a new life. But I'm an adventurer. I take risks," Larry says.

"Yes, that may be true, but you are hurting me and the children so much. I love you. They love you. We just finished building the house. How can you leave us all?" Diana replies with a shaking voice.

"I have to understand the nature of the universe," Larry says. Diana says nothing because she doesn't know how to respond. It's almost as if he's saying to you "I did it. I'm a big boy now. You can't control me."

"Yes, I'm living in a loft. It's the honest, courageous thing to do. I found my soul mate. Still, it may not work," Walt says.

Beth is jolted to the core when she hears "It may not work." She thinks, "The kids and I are suffering so. He has created this terrible upheaval and he's saying 'It may not work.' What will he do if it doesn't work? Just come back like nothing happened? But we've already started to sell the house. The kids are probably going to have to change schools next year because I can't afford to live in this neighborhood anymore. I'm going to have to take a full-time job. Doesn't he realize what he's done?"

But Beth only says "What do you mean, 'It may not work'?"

Walt says nothing, but what he means is, "The Script told me that saying 'I'm a risk taker' sounds good. But along with taking risks I've got to hedge my bets, financially and emotionally. I've already put some money away. Now I've got to hedge my bets emotionally. So I'm asking you to reassure me that you'll be my safety net.

I want to hear you say, 'Walt, if it doesn't work, I'll be waiting for you.'"

Walt cannot say out loud what he means because the Script has told him to stick with the heroic image of courage and risk taking. What Walt does actually say is, "I'm willing to go forth into the unknown and see where it takes me."

Beth will find out soon that before Walt set out he knew exactly where it was taking him. Someone else was already in place. But now Beth says nothing. You can't win against God, courage, and risk taking.

Beth can't help thinking to herself that it would have been more courageous if Walt had directly confronted her before he took such a drastic step.

TIP: EXPOSE HIS COVER.

He has wrapped himself in God, courage, and risk taking. But clothes *don't* make the man.

If you try to pull off his cover in a direct conversation with him he will only keep wrapping it tighter. But know that your instincts are right—underneath the cover is not courage and risk taking. Just the opposite. He has taken the name of the Lord and courage in vain.

SCENE 10: GOING PUBLIC WITH THE MISTRESS

Steve and Bill are sitting in the Denver Mile High Flyers Club lounge waiting for a delayed flight. Exhausted from three long days of meetings, Steve says to Bill, "I wish I could look forward to getting back after these three days, but I'll tell you I can't really look forward to what I come home to. Complain, complain, complain, and the old lady's always 'too tired.' I don't even know what to do about the company retreat next month. Audrey has gained so much weight, and you've heard the guys laughing about fat women. I don't know if I can bring her."

Bill responds, "That bad, huh?"

Cliff is standing in his office doorway talking to his secretary, Priscilla. "Priscilla, I wonder, could you take care of getting my mother hooked up with the senior center program in her neighborhood? I tell you I've asked Brenda a thousand times and it never seems to get done. I don't know what's wrong with her."

"Don't worry, Cliff, I'll be happy to take care of that for your mother. I understand what you have to go through with Brenda. She sure doesn't make things easy for you."

It's four-thirty on a Thursday afternoon and Josh feels he just has to take a break from the mountains of reports he has on his desk. He wanders out of his office and over to Christine's. Christine always has a sympathetic ear. He can tell her anything and she just seems to understand.

"How's it going, Christine?" Josh says.

"Oh the usual," Christine replies.

"Yeah, the usual," Josh says. "That's probably what I'll hear at home too. I tell you Anna must sit at her job all day making lists of things for me to do. You know our sex life isn't that great either. She treats me like 'bring home the bacon and leave me alone.'"

"Oh, Josh, that's terrible."

. . .

For months or maybe years before he has taken a mistress, he has been telling people that his wife doesn't treat him well, doesn't understand him, and is really crazy. He chooses people to confide in who he feels will be sympathetic. Maybe he knows or senses that this person has similar feelings about his or her own marriage. Or it might be someone who likes to hear usually private details about someone else's life. Or maybe it's someone who feels flattered that he is confiding in her in this way; or who has a personal or business reason to want to flatter him with interested attention. Sometimes he may even choose a complete stranger to confide the most intimate details of his sex life.

These people give him no back talk, don't dispute what he says, and add support and justification to his feelings of unhappiness. "If Bill and Priscilla and Christine agree with me about how difficult my wife is, then I am fully justified in finding fault with her and going for the happiness I deserve."

It is in this state of readiness that he found his "soul mate." But now, after he has dropped the Bomb, he has work to do. Just as he planned for months how to drop the Bomb, he has been planning for months how to introduce his mistress into society. It's been very strenuous because he has had to work in secret, and therefore couldn't call upon anyone to help him—he had only the Script he's memorized and his success file of other men's stories to go on. But once he's dropped the Bomb, it's inevitable that he has to take the next step.

He asks himself, "Who do I want to be the first to see her? Who do I want to send out the first wave of rumors? In what setting will she fit best?" He might not have to go to quite the lengths

Prince Charles did when introducing Camilla, but he still orchestrates it carefully. He introduces her first to those people who are on his side, people he has told repeatedly that his wife doesn't treat him well. As he introduces the new woman, he makes it clear that she makes him very happy.

"Christine, do you and Ryan have time for a drink after work tomorrow or do you have to get back to the kids? I'd like you to meet the new special woman in my life. I know you'll love Kitty. She makes me so happy. Anna and I had really drifted apart long ago," Josh says.

Christine thinks about this for a second. She knew Josh had been telling her for quite a while that Anna really didn't treat him well, didn't appreciate him. She figures they're finally splitting up. But she's surprised to hear about another woman. Still, she likes Josh and wants to be part of whatever is happening in his life so she says, "Sure, Ryan and I would love to have a drink with you tomorrow."

As Larry stands squeezed in the back of the elevator to his forty-second-floor office on a busy Monday morning, he sees Josh rushing to push himself into the last spot before the doors close. Larry thinks to himself that he hasn't seen Josh since he left MondaBank over a year ago and he shouts out, "Hey guy, what're you up to now? Haven't seen you in ages." Josh replies, "I'm at Wetherby Frisch now. I moved upstairs to be COO. What about you?"

Larry replies, "Keepin' busy. You know Monda, always involved in something."

Josh says, "Hey, let's have dinner, you and Cindy. I want you to meet my fiancée. We're getting married next month. You know Anna and I split up."

Larry is silent for a moment, because for the last fifteen years he had only known Josh to talk about his wife and their four children. Then he says to Josh, "I'll give you a buzz."

Larry doesn't respond for a couple of weeks because he's not sure what to do. Then he decides he has to pick up the phone to make the uncomfortable call he has been avoiding. "Hi Josh. It's Larry. Just wanted to get back to you about dinner. You know I did mention it to Cindy and she was really concerned about Anna. She sees Anna when they chaperone the fourth-grade trips."

"Larry, she doesn't need to worry about Anna. She's doing fine. And wait 'til you meet Kitty. You'll both love her."

"Well, let me get back to you Josh."

On this Friday afternoon Josh doesn't return to his office from lunch until 4:00 P.M. His secretary, Bonnie, is seriously concerned about where he is when he walks in slowly with a woman close by his side.

"Bonnie, I'd like you to meet Kitty, the new woman in my life," Josh says. He has been thinking, "This is all I have to say and Bonnie will understand what has happened. She has been my secretary for so long and she knows what I've been through with Anna. Bonnie will kind of let everybody in the office know in a nice, easy way."

"Oh, pleased to meet you," Bonnie says.

. . .

Wherever he introduces Kitty he says or strongly implies that he just met Kitty. If he told the truth—that he's known Kitty for two years and has been having "is is" sex with her for over a year—then he would have been an adulterer and deceitful to his friends, which is not the kind of man he is. "Even if some of my friends eventually find out that I had known Kitty for a while, first, they'll realize that Anna 'drove me to it,' that Anna 'never treated me well,' that Anna 'didn't understand me,' that Kitty makes me so happy, and that there is no question that 'I deserve my happiness.' Secondly, they'll never mention it to me directly: they'll asume I was fully justified in doing whatever I did because I have made it clear how Anna didn't treat me well, she's really crazy, and she was never the right person for me. It wasn't a loving relationship, but they'll all see how loving Kitty is."

All his careful planning pays off. His mistress, soon to be his new wife, is accepted by most of his business associates and the friends he has chosen to introduce her to.

SCENE 11: "IT'S YOUR RESPONSIBILITY TO KEEP THINGS CIVIL AND NICE"

It's working out well for him so far. Just the way he planned it. We're in Act II, Scene 11. But he senses just a small tinge of anger in your voice, of disagreement; you mentioned getting your own lawyer; you said something about needing more money. So he has to cement his "victory," make sure he stays in control. In previous scenes, following the Script he has learned so well, he established that the original sins and blame were yours. Now he has to establish that the burden is on you to make up for this and not to make things worse. After all, it's the least he can expect from you to make up for all the misery you caused him. Now that he's found the solution to his problem, he's not going to let you mess it up.

So he is "living alone in a cabin in the woods" but he does manage to get to town to make a call.

HUSBAND: Everything will be okay if you don't get bitter. We can just work things out between us.

WIFE: Well, I guess we can. But I don't know. What do you mean by okay?

HUSBAND: Things don't have to get nasty. It's your responsibility to keep things civil and nice.

WIFE: Well, I don't think it can be nice with what you've done.

HUSBAND: Well, civil.

You're feeling confused, baffled, and wondering who belongs in the asylum. How could he be saying that it's *your* responsibility to keep things civil and nice? He's the one who was unfaithful, who broke his vows to you, who has inflicted hurt on you and your children. He just acted most uncivil and really, really not nice.

You think, "Isn't it mostly *his* responsibility to be civil and nice?" Everything you've learned since childhood is that the one who committed the crime is the one who has the responsibility to right the wrong, to make up to those he harmed. You've learned that this is true whether the crime is murder or the crime is seven-year-old Adam stepping on his playmate Eric's toy and breaking it. If the crime is murder, the best the perpetrator can do is to ask for forgiveness and serve time in jail. If it's breaking the toy, we expect Adam to apologize and to do his best to fix or replace the toy.

Based on all the values, beliefs, and expectations you've lived by your entire life, what he's saying doesn't make any sense.

.   .   .

chorus tells you you're supposed to be nice regard-
of how you feel, how anyone else has acted toward
and what the circumstances are, because it will be
r for everyone that way. "Easier for everyone." Does
nclude you? You're confused, baffled, and wonder-
people really understand what has happened to you
ur family.

easy. It's hard, and maybe not even a good idea, to
to someone who has lied, cheated, acted totally
e to your interests, and shown not a whiff of car-
ou and your children. But once you know that
st part of the Script, you will be less confused.

really clear how many behaviors are forbidden to you
keep things civil and nice, Scene 11 will also feature
e:

ne big louse to do this to me. Who is that filthy
re seeing? How could you do that?

hing will be fine if you don't get bitter.

" 'If I don't get bitter'? But I do feel angry, and bit-
t fall on me to keep the bad emotions out of this?
maybe I shouldn't be feeling bitter. Maybe I don't
cept life as it comes. Maybe I don't know how to
judgmental person. I certainly don't want people
e the way they talk about Ginny—'Oh, Ginny,
bitter woman.' Okay, I won't get bitter. I'll be re-

o hear:

Let's look at another example from childhood. (It's no accident that going back to children's behavior is so useful: first, because in many ways he's acting like a child; and second, because the values and beliefs you're going by now stretch back to codes of behavior you started learning in childhood.) If five-year-old Sam says, "I want to take all of Billy's toys to my house and keep them and not give Billy any of my toys," his father and mother will say, "No, you can't do that." The parents know it's not right and there will be consequences. Billy's mother may never let Billy play with Sam again and may accuse you and Sam of stealing. But Sam says, "I want to take all of Billy's toys!" You know that no matter what you say, Sam will persist in saying, "I want to do it. Why can't I?" You will never get through because as a five-year-old Sam doesn't have the same values and expectations you do. His values are not all developed and understood yet. You know you will never get a five-year-old to understand why he can't take all of Billy's toys. He's talking nonsense because he is a child.

It's the same with the cheating man. He is talking nonsense and you will never make sense of it. The difference between the cheating man and the child is that the unfaithful man was talking sense and now all of a sudden he is talking nonsense. (The "all of a sudden" coincides with when you know for sure he is cheating and he knows you know.) With the child we all know and accept that children say nonsensical things.

You still wonder if you are lacking in intelligence and an understanding of what is sense and what is nonsense. Nonsense! Your understanding makes perfect sense.

TIP: DON'T TRY TO MAKE SENSE OF NONSENSE. NOBODY CAN.

Not only has he learned his Script lines well, he has had reinforcement from hearing the Script over and over from other men and the popular media. His more sophisticated friends have even provided refinement to the Script when needed by alerting him to the latest nuances.

This reinforcement is coming at you, too, from millions of supporting actors in the chorus singing songs from *Manners and Mores for Girls*, a play in the Popular Wisdom and Culture series. *Manners and Mores for Girls* is a complete guide but it never spells out the fact that men can be either naughty or nice, and win anyway, but if women are too nice they usually lose. And losing means lifelong losses such as a substantially reduced standard of living and less time with your children.

It started when you were about two years old and you were told to "make nice" to the puppy next door and "make nice" to the little boy across the street.

It continued with the admonition to be nice to your friends, be nice (and respectful) to your teachers, be nice (and loving) to your grandparents, be nice (and charming) to the proprietor of the candy store (he may give you a piece of candy), be nice to your neighbors, be nice to your boss (you may be the one to get a raise).

And most everything you've heard and read—from Ann Landers to *Parents* magazine to the family column in the *Wall Street Journal* to the Bible—says that the children, and you too, will do better if everybody is amiable, if you

don't let things get contentious, if
cheek, if everyone is *civil* and *nic*
think the burden is mostly on *yo*
ing the Script. The chorus starte
popular wisdom in Act I with th
"Civil and Nice" regaling the i
always civil and nice. He has
now they have become his ow

The lines of "Civil and Nice"

"Isn't it wonderful how Pe
get along even though he l
with Carrie?"

"I saw them all at the Ki
just seem to love Carrie

"Peggy's a really big p
Tom and just make su
It's easier on everyo

"Peggy and Tom's k
two families to lov

"Everybody acts

"It's so nice to be

The pressure is
recall the word
Coming to Tov
nice."

(It's no coin

The
less
you,
easie
that
ing if
and y

It's no
be nice
opposit
ing for
this is ju

To make it
in order to
this exchang

WIFE: You are o
woman you a

HUSBAND: Every

And you think
ter. Why does
But then again
know how to a
be an open, non
to talk about m
she's just an old
ally nice."

In Scene 11 we al

WIFE: Why didn't you pick up the children at six o'clock the way you promised? I missed half of the evening with my friends. I'm so angry with you.

HUSBAND: For heaven's sake, get yourself under control.

WIFE: What do you mean "under control"? Where were you?

HUSBAND: I have things to do. I can't always be here just on the minute.

WIFE: Just on the minute? You were two hours late.

HUSBAND: Simmer down. Get yourself under control. And while we're talking about it, get that wild-eyed lawyer of yours under control too.

And you think, " 'under control'? Am I not supposed to be angry if you show up two hours late and you ruin my one evening out? Why am I the one who has to stay under control? But then again maybe I overreacted. Maybe my outburst *was* out of control. Maybe that's not the way a mature adult should react. I certainly don't want people to talk about me the way they talk about Marci—'Oh, Marci, she's just a raving maniac when she talks to Tim.' Okay, I'll control myself. I'll be really nice."

Of course he wants you to be nice. He won't have to deal with your anger. It will also keep you from mentioning anything he might have done that's *not* nice. It wouldn't be nice of you to bring that up! If he can get your lawyer to be nice too, that will be even nicer because then he's more likely to get a good settlement. The scene he planned in his head in Act I is you and your lawyer (actually he was thinking it will be even *nicer* if he can get you not to have any lawyer) will be really nice, will shut up (see Act II, Scene 12) and you can all walk away still friends (see Act II, Scene 13). Still friends for the foursome involved here—you, him, your lawyer, and his lawyer—means every one of the four walks away "still friends" with every other one of the four, especially you and him and especially the two lawyers with each other. If you're nice, it's also easier for him to control the end result—a nicer cut. Your being nice will be the kindest, nicest cut of all—for *him*. He cuts a deal to keep most of the money.

TIP: ADD MORE SPICE

Think back to the nursery rhyme:

Sugar and spice and everything nice
That's what little girls are made of.
Then . . . ADD MORE SPICE!

Your best attitude recipe now is a perfect balance between sugar and spice. And the spice we mean is fiery hot pepper. He would like to keep the two of you together for just one more big recipe that balances out this way: You're all sugar and he's all spice. But you've got both ingredients inside of you, and you can make your own perfect recipe. He's trying to get you off balance. If he can get you to go light on the spice, his recipe will come out better.

What this means in practice is that you have to watch your attitude in every interaction with him. If you add too much spice then you're "the bitch who no man could possibly live with." If you add too much sugar then he's got his recipe set so that your bread will never rise.

We recommend combining two sources to get a superior blend of fiery hot pepper: first what is in your own mental cupboard, and then the best of the imports—your lawyer.

Following this spicy tip will enable you to thoroughly appreciate his lines in the finale, when the unexpected amount of spice is causing him indigestion and he says, "This is not the way I planned it."

SCENE 12: "IF YOU'D JUST SHUT UP, EVERYTHING WOULD BE OKAY"

HUSBAND: Why do we have to disagree about this? I know what I want and we can just sit down and work it all out.

WIFE: But I don't see how I'm going to manage with no money.

HUSBAND: I told you I'm going to take care of you.

WIFE: But I just want some assurances here. I don't know what's happening.

HUSBAND: Don't worry about it. You don't need to know what's happening. It'll all be fine.

WIFE: Well, right now it's not fine. I need to talk to you about all this stuff.

HUSBAND: If you'd just shut up, everything would be okay.

You're aghast at his putting the responsibility on you again, the responsibility not just to be civil and nice but now to be civil and nice *and* to shut up. He's getting more and more unreasonable. Yet *he's* the one who cheated, who walked out, who's sleeping with another woman. But remember, he's just following the Script.

The Script is that you, the little lady, should be accepting of everything. After all, it's your fault to begin with. You didn't understand him, didn't love him enough. Now that everybody has recognized these "facts" and that he deserves the true happiness he has found, things will naturally fall into place and he will get this finished in a civil way. After the difficult years he's endured with you, people will realize all attention has to be on him and his needs have to take center stage.

So everyone needs to shut up and listen to how it's going to be.

TIP: OPEN YOUR MOUTH AND CLOSE YOUR EARS. DON'T SHUT UP.

This is a reversal of the old adage, probably written by a man to be followed by a woman, that says close your mouth and open your ears and listen up. In other words, you can't listen if you're talking.

Reversals are very helpful when dealing with a man who's following the Script. Face your head in the opposite direction from where he's trying to get it to go. He wants your head a little bowed in penance for the unhappiness you've caused him, nodding sweetly in assent to what he's done, eyes gazing on him with acceptance, lips smiling nicely with no words spewing forth except "yes," and all ears to what he's telling you.

We recommend reversing this. Hold your head high, listen little to what he says, look carefully and dispassionately at his actions, and speak up.

Your natural instinct tells you that if you speak up, he will get angry and act even worse toward you. Besides your hurt and fear and sadness, you don't want to have to deal with someone who is angry with you. It would seem that being pleasant and nice and agreeable would gain you his future help and support, which you feel you still want and need. You think that if you do what he tells you to do (right now that would be to shut up), he will be appreciative and will be nice to you in return. Not so. He will, in fact, respect you for standing up, not shutting up.

TIP: BUY THE "SIMON SAYS" VIDEO

Throw a wrench into the Script. He is going back to adolescent behavior, acting like a teenager in love. He's also going back to elementary school games. Remember "Simon Says"? No coincidence Simon is a man. Simon tries to confuse you by saying one thing and doing another. The children's game is, you win if you do what he says and not what he does.

He wants and expects you to act like a child. "Listen to me. Do what I say and don't contradict and don't ask any questions"—just the way children are expected to obey their parents.

But the way to win the adult game is to go by what he *does*, not what he *says*.

SCENE 13: DOING THINGS THE OPPOSITE OF THE WAY HE'S ALWAYS DONE THEM

Sarah has just sat down with a latte in The Little Red Coffeehouse hoping for a break while her toddler is occupied with a cookie, when she spies her friend Alana walking in with her five-year-old twins. "Hi, Alana, come have a seat with me," she calls out, as Alana turns her way. Sarah thinks it's no wonder Alana looks so drawn and tired with Stan having left her and the four kids so recently. When Alana sits down with her coffee Sarah says, "The twins seem to grow an inch a week. How're you doing?"

Alana answers, "Good and bad. I was doing better 'til I found out that Stan just met someone and he just moved in with her."

"The same woman he's been seeing all along?" Sarah asks.

"What do you mean? He told me he just met her," Alana says.

"I hate to tell you this," Sarah says, "but he's been running around with her for more than a year."

"What? Stan swore to me he just met her."

"Don't believe it," Sarah says, thinking back to when she first saw Stan leaving an intimate restaurant with a woman a year ago. "He's not telling you the truth."

Alana is stunned. She can't believe her husband has lied to her when the truth was always so important to him. She thinks back to a time not that long ago when the family was all sitting around the dinner table. Stan was telling them about his difficult day. "I had to confront one of the tech people when he out-and-out lied to me about why he was late for work." Alana and the four children listened closely as Stan went on, "He told me that a car hit a cow out in the county before he got on the interstate. I believed him until I found out he told someone else that what really happened was that he had locked his keys in the car the night before. And to make it worse, he was saying how proud he was that he had pulled off the lie."

At this point thirteen-year-old Matt asked, "So what'd you do, Dad?"

Stan said, "I did what I had to do. I told him I cannot tolerate lying and if it happens again, he's out the door."

Now that she hears that Stan has been secretly seeing another woman and never told her, she is confused and baffled. "Stan was always so fastidious about the obligation to tell the truth. He always told the kids, 'I'll never be angry if you tell me the truth, but if you lie, that's wrong and then I'll be angry.' How could he say one thing just a few months ago, and his whole life long, and now have done something totally different? What does he mean? Is it possible that Sarah's information is wrong and he wasn't seeing someone else behind my back?" Alana wonders. "Stan is such a good person. I don't know what to think."

DAVE: The kids can make their own way through college. Why do they need to go to college at all? Anyway, I'm not giving them money for college. So that's it.

DARIA: But we always said we would help them as much as we could! Remember when I asked how we would pay for it if Kelly got into Harvard, and you said the money was there? You told me not to worry, she could go to the best college she could get into. Even though we're apart, you and I have enough money to help them. You said you never wanted to be like Bud. You called him stingy when he told his kids they're on their own for college when he's got tons of money.

DAVE: That's different.

Daria says nothing because she's asked Dave before how it was different and he always answers very abruptly. "It's different. Can't you see that?" But even though she says nothing, confusing thoughts are roiling in her mind. She just can't figure out how Dave can reconcile calling Bud stingy when he could afford to help his kids with college but didn't, and then do what he's doing now. He's doing the same thing but saying it's different and implying that what he's doing is fine. Daria is also wondering if it is her thinking that is weak because she cannot see the difference. Dave makes it seem like it's so obvious that any child would understand it. He's implying that if Daria doesn't understand, there is something wrong with her.

"Is it just me," you may wonder, "or does every woman feel this way?"

We'll say it again: Every woman feels this way.

Know that there is nothing wrong with your thinking. Your understanding is perfect. But now that he has been unfaithful (which he will usually acknowledge only indirectly if at all), now that he's not putting family first, "That's Different."

You're trying to play by the rules of the game you and your husband have always played by—the rules he has always said he is playing by. But you have to recognize that he's now playing a different game with different rules. You can't figure out what's happening. The new game makes you look crazy, makes you think you're crazy. You can never win if you don't know the rules of the game he's playing.

HUSBAND: It's no wonder I had to leave you. Traveling is part of my work. I had to be away for a couple of weeks at a time. I needed to visit our other offices. And you couldn't be with me on every trip.

WIFE: But that doesn't mean you had to cheat. There are plenty of men who travel a lot for their work and they're not cheating. What about Andy? He's in London all the time. What about Brian? Going all over visiting factories. They're not cheating.

HUSBAND: That's different.

Men at the highest levels are sometimes doing the opposite of what they've said are their most strongly held values. Jack Welch, possibly the most admired CEO of recent times, has been lauded for his principles and his guidance to others. In an op-ed piece about leadership in *The Wall Street Journal*, Jack Welch wrote that a key question in evaluating a leader is "Does he demonstrate fairness, loyalty, goodness, compassion?" Yet when he left his wife of almost thirteen years in 2002 he demonstrated none of the above.

Even the beloved and respected Dr. Spock, who was the spokesperson for family values and a strong family ethic, in his own life did the opposite of what he said he believed in. He was very clear in interviews about what he believed: "I think the most important value by far is to bring up children excited about helping other people, first in their family and then other people outside." "I think that the Golden Rule—treating other people with the same respect you expect for yourself—is the basis of every religious or spiritual value system the world has ever known." "You need to be thinking of the other person, not just of yourself. I think we need to bring in the spiritual aspects that marriage is not for personal gratification, it is wanting to live the rest of your life with somebody, helping them, and raising fine children." Yet he divorced his wife, Jane, after forty-eight years of marriage. Just one year later he married a woman forty years younger than he.

It is not much mentioned because of his role in the aftermath of September 11, but New York City Mayor Rudolph Guiliani was also saying one thing in public and doing exactly the opposite when it came to his own family. Guiliani was leading the world in mourning the dead firemen and policemen who left thousands of fatherless children—urging all Americans to help these children retain the home life they had been accustomed to. At the same time he had fired his wife, the mother of his children, as first lady after she had obtained a restraining order against his mistress to prevent the adulterous relationship in the children's home, Gracie Mansion.

TIP: BUY "THE I AM KING JAMES BIBLE"

Sometime in Act I he quietly switched Bibles on you. It was subtle and silent and extremely difficult to detect. You're reading and going by the Bible (you may call it commandments or code of ethics or sense of right and wrong) that you've always gone by. He always said he was going by the same Bible. He even spoke before the Chamber of Commerce about what this Bible said. His topic was "How Loyalty Brings Success at Work and at Home." He spoke from this Bible at the church dinner, waxing expansive on "Living by the Golden Rule in All Relationships." And he spoke at his company's nation-wide "Ethical Values in Business" meeting, saying that the best businesspeople actually put family values first.

But then this Bible became very heavy, a burden to carry around. Following the definitions of right and wrong described in this book weren't making things go his way anymore. He saw that some other men were going by a different Bible and getting what they wanted. So he switched to the new good book, "The I AM KING James Bible." It's a very practical Bible with many choices. What it all boils down to is "do whatever works, whatever makes you happy." And since the disciples of this Bible are all Kings, they decide which commandments rule the land. These unfaithful Kings (well, they're faithful in some ways but unfaithful in others—which is another thing that's confusing you) are all following the

Script. They choose a code that synthesizes the spiritual, courageous, and honest with what makes them happy. A little of the old and a little of the new.

You start to think you must be remembering things wrong. Either you're misremembering the Bible you thought you both lived by—maybe it *did* say that if this Bible isn't getting you what you want it's okay to switch?—or you're misremembering the code he said he lived by. You think you're losing your mind—that he's making sense and you're just not grasping it. You think maybe he's right that he's different and you're just not understanding the differences.

But you're not losing your mind and you're not stupid. We're in Act II, Scene 13, and he's following the Script.

You might start to notice that even in small and insignificant areas he is doing things the opposite way of the way he has always done them. He always said he hated going to the movies. Now he says he loves the movies. He always said fancy sports cars were a waste of money. Now he has the raciest car he can afford. He always said he would not dress up like a penguin to attend a charity dinner. Now he has three different tuxedos and goes to several dinners a month. He always said he had to live no more than half a mile from his office. Now he lives an hour's commute away. He always said that men with long hair looked like peacocks. Now his hair is so long that it spills down the back of his jacket.

It's a hot summer's day and Gloria and Marie, both recently divorced from their doctor husbands, are walking across the vast lawn of the county fairgrounds toward the local artist exhibits of the county fair. When Marie passes the charity section and sees a booth for Africa Against AIDS, she says to Gloria, "Remember how the guys volunteered every year to treat children in Africa?"

Gloria says, "Yes, they sacrificed a lot to do that and they did a good job."

Just then they catch a glimpse of two men ahead of them who look like they just stepped out of the yacht club dining room. "Gee, look who that is," Gloria says. "Our dearly departed Steve and Jerry. Cashmere sweaters tied around their shoulders no less. And Fianicci loafers and no socks. Did they ever dress like that before, Marie?"

"No, they didn't, Gloria. Not so long ago they were Doctors Without Borders. Now they are Doctors Without Socks."

SCENE 14: IT HAPPENS ALL THE TIME

"Oh gosh, Phil, how could you leave us? I love you, the kids love you. Breaking up the family is terrible. You don't know how hurt my parents are, and worried. They think it's awful that the kids will grow up without a father. Just the thought of divorce makes me sick to my stomach. I don't know how I'll carry on. Who's going to play ball with little Jimmy? Who's going to cheer Francie on in her soccer games? I'm devastated. What will the neighbors think? They always thought we had such a happy family."

"Margie, it happens all the time. You're carrying on so. The kids will do fine. I'll still play ball with Jimmy. I'll still go to Francie's soccer games. You'll get along fine. Everything will be the same."

You can't believe what he said. It Happens All the Time. You were already feeling hurt, angry, sad, devastated, worried, and embarrassed. Now you feel baffled and confused about one more thing he's uttered. How can he take such a devastating event for the family and make it into something so ordinary, something that "happens all the time"?

You ask yourself, "Is he right? Am I making a big deal out of nothing? Am I making it worse for the kids by showing how hurt I am? Maybe everything *will* be the same.

"He seems so calm, so contented. Didn't I mean anything to him? If he thinks nothing of any significance has happened, I guess I don't mean a thing to him. I always thought our marriage was something."

It's a few weeks after George has moved out and he's coming to pick up the kids. George walks into the kitchen where Irene is wiping up and says, "Hi, Irene, how are you doing?"

Irene answers, "Well, struggling along. It's hard."

George is annoyed to hear this "complaining" answer and says, "Irene, you've got to move on."

You're confused. He's telling you Nothing Happened. But every religious and civil code you've ever known says Something Did Happen. You heard the crash as the stone tablet fell in pieces to the ground. It was the sound of the tablet that says "adultery is wrong" being knocked over. These broken covenants make a very loud noise to you. But he says he doesn't hear anything. And some of your friends tell you you're making a big deal out of a little noise. And anyway they don't want to know about it because then the noise may start to resonate in their own lives.

You are receiving both individual and societal messages that say Nothing Happened.

He says things to you like "We can still be friends," which implies that nothing happened. If you act like nothing happened, people respond to you better and they applaud you for not being angry, for being nice to him and to the other woman. People are constantly "moving you on," implying that your separation or divorce is a minor event in life that you just have to put behind you. They imply it is no more significant than the disappointment in having the sofa you ordered in blue arrive in green. "Is it just me," you may wonder, "or does every woman feel this way?" Every woman feels this way.

"Hi, Veronica, how's it going?" Rita calls to her friend across the aisle in the supermarket. "Are you still in the house on Rainbow Road?"

"No, Rita, we had to move. It just wasn't going to work out to stay there. We moved to Stillwell Lane."

"Oh, how nice. You and the kids doing well? I'm so glad you're not into that angry venting and carrying on. Just take it nice and easy. It'll all work out fine. Bob's the kind of guy who wouldn't let you down."

Veronica walks away from this chance encounter with Rita feeling worse. "If I tell Rita that I am angry and do need a chance to vent, and that Bob did let me down, she won't want to hear it," Veronica thinks. "Something *did* happen to me, but I can see that people react better if I pretend that nothing happened. If I pretend I'm not hurt, that Bob and I get along very well, that the kids are doing fine, that my life hasn't really changed, that I'm moving on."

HEIDI: Oh, Yvonne, good to see you. You weren't at the parents' meeting at the school last week, were you?

YVONNE: No, I just wasn't up to it. It's been really hard since Will left. I'm trying to be there for the kids but a lot of the time I'm just sitting at the kitchen table crying. And the kids miss Will so much.

HEIDI: They'll get over it. You will too.

YVONNE: Well, I don't know. One minute I'm furious with Will for his betrayal, the next minute I'm sobbing, and the next minute he's on the phone acting like nothing happened.

HEIDI: Look, you gotta move on. All that crying isn't going to do you any good.

YVONNE: I feel so hurt and sad. And I don't even know where my next dollar is coming from. How could Will do this to me?

HEIDI: Well, I've got to be running along. Take it easy.

Heidi hurries away thinking to herself, "Gosh, doesn't Yvonne know how to get over it and move on? Who needs angry, weepy people like that?"

No fault divorce laws convey society's message that nobody did anything for which they should or will be faulted. In other words, nothing happened. It is ironic and sad that in any county courthouse in America in one room a judge may be performing a marriage ceremony along with the sacred vows—for sure, *something* is *happening*—and just down the hall in another courtroom a judge may be presiding over a no fault divorce saying "nothing happened."

In contrast, there are many messages you receive that say something *did* happen. First, marriage is a legally and religiously recognized state. The idea of getting married, the marriage ceremony itself, and wedding anniversaries are times for hearty congratulations and expansive celebration. For instance, it has been reported that after the purchase of a home the next largest expenditure in a couple's lifetime is their wedding. Therefore marriage is obviously *something*. It follows that when it breaks apart, it can't be *nothing*.

If a marriage breaks apart, there are again many messages that say something did happen. Your feelings are different. You feel hurt, angry, sad, ashamed, embarrassed, anxious, and tired. Your children may have the same feelings. People treat you differently. There is a lot of new paperwork. You check a different box when a form asks if you are single, married, divorced, or widowed. The court is involved in your life. You have to adjust to doing with less. For sure, something did happen.

TIP: IT HAPPENS ALL THE TIME

The sad fact is that, on the surface, there is some truth to what he said—divorce does happen a lot. But the inner message he hopes to convey with this line is false!

The cover story he hopes to get across is:

If it's nothing, then it's normal. And if it's normal, it's nothing. Therefore he did nothing wrong.

Don't accept it. Acknowledge your feelings of sorrow, hurt, anger, and fear. Something did happen, and it's no wonder you feel that way.

Watch Out for Friends Who Make You Feel Worse.

At this time especially you need to be around people who will let you express your feelings and not cut you off. Pay attention to how you feel after you leave your friends. Do you feel better or do you feel worse?

Friends should acknowledge and validate what you feel, make you feel strong and capable, and not belittle you or imply that you did something wrong or in some way deserved it.

SCENE 15: TAKING SOMETHING OF NO VALUE

Stephie has some neighbors coming over for coffee and goes to her kitchen cabinet to take out some mugs. She has always kept the good mugs in the front of the cabinet and the old, chipped mugs in the back, all laid out in neat rows. As she's pulling out the matching mugs and putting them on a tray, she notices an empty space in the row of old mugs. She thinks to herself, "Why would there be a space there? That's really odd. Did one of the kids take an old mug to mix watercolors in? Did the plumber take one to grab a drink of water when he was here fixing the sink?" She decides she has no time to worry about it now because her guests are about to arrive.

A few days later when she is again looking into the cabinet with the mugs, Stephie wonders if maybe Bruce took a couple of the old mugs when he was in the house bringing Jenny and Rachel back from their weekend with him. She has noticed that whenever Bruce is back in the house, he stays longer than he really has to and spends time just looking around as if he were coming back to his childhood home and recalling old memories. So when Bruce comes again to pick up the girls on Saturday morning, Stephie asks him, "Bruce, do you know what happened to those old mugs with the astrology signs that I kept in the back of the kitchen cabinet?"

Bruce seems startled for a second, then answers, "Yes, I took them for my house because I want them."

Stephie is mystified as to why Bruce would want two cracked, chipped mugs, but she says nothing.

Larry moved out a year ago but Connie has called him to help her move some heavy things in the garage. Even though Larry has re-married, he comes over every few weeks just to chat and almost always says "yes" if Connie needs help with something. After a couple of hours, Larry has finished moving the heavy stuff around. They both go into the house to wash up. Then Larry sits down at the kitchen table with a cup of coffee. Connie sees that he has placed a box on the table. On the top of the box is a picture of the Virgin Islands. They picked it up on a trip ten years earlier. Connie asks, "What do you have that box on the table for?"

Larry answers, "Oh, it's just something I want."

Connie says, "Why?" and Larry answers "I just want it."

It's completely baffling. Why would he want something so trivial, so old and beat up, something with absolutely no value? It is especially difficult to figure out when just a short time ago he was so eager to leave you and the children and his home to move in with his mistress.

We can predict that a man who has left his family and the home you shared will, if he has the opportunity, take something of no monetary value. Sometimes he will take it and tell you about it later, sometimes he will mention it at the time. He may never tell you at all, and you may never notice.

He has two lives—his first life and his second life. Nobody in his second life knows much about or is very interested in his first life. His wife and his children from his first life also have little knowledge or interest in his second life. These small, seemingly insignificant things of no monetary value actually do have a value to him—they are a thread tying his first life to his second.

SCENE 16: MIXED MESSAGES

"He said I'm a terrible mother? Is that what Steve said?" Amy can't believe what Diana is relating to her. "But just last week he told me himself that I was a very good mother."

Diana had just told Amy what Steve was telling Diana's husband, Ted, and some of the guys in the Seacon tech department at the company retreat last weekend. Ted said to Diana that Amy must not be the kind of mother she appeared to be because Steve was standing around telling the guys that all these years Amy was just not there for the kids.

"Oh, Amy," Diana says, "Steve must not have meant it that way. He knows you're a good mother. Maybe the guys were just standing around grousing to each other. Even though he's not living here anymore he knows how much time you spend with the kids. Aren't the two of us just always in our cars taking a bunch of kids somewhere?"

Amy thinks, "We sure are. So why is Steve saying I'm not there for the kids?" She says to Diana, "Oh, Diana, why is he saying one thing one week and another thing the next? It doesn't make any sense."

It's parents' night at Adam's and Will's school and Amy is rushing to get there on time. She thinks to herself that this is the fourth time she's been at the school that day—once to drop the kids off, once to pick them up, and once for a meeting with the other hockey team parents. Amy arrives just on time and follows the prescribed route from classroom to classroom, listening to all the teachers describe the school year so far. Then she's off to the reception in the gym. Since Steve moved out she's never sure which of the kids' events he will come to, but there he is striding across the gym floor in her direction.

"Hi, Amy," Steve says. "Have you been to all the boys' classes?"

"Yes, I have," Amy answers. "And it's my fourth time here today."

"Well, the other moms and dads sure like you. You're a wonderful mother. Mike told me that if not for you the hockey tournament would never have happened because the parents were bickering so badly. He said you got everybody to get along and focus on the end result for the kids."

"That's nice of Mike to say that," Amy replies. Her voice sounds calm but her mind is spinning with confusion and frustration because of Steve's contradictory statements. He told the Seacon guys she was a terrible mother but now he tells her she's a wonderful mother.

.   .   .

Steve and the boys have arrived in Vermont ski country for the weekend and even though it will only be light for another hour they head straight for the slopes.

"You boys look great. Those are just the skis and boots I wanted you to have. Timmy's dad told me they're the latest and you'll go faster that way. There're some downhill events for the younger kids here this weekend at Stowe and you should do very well."

"Yes, Mom could only find them at SkiHigh and she was wondering whether to buy them because she said they sure were expensive but we told her it's what all the kids have."

"Yes, it's the right thing. Just the right equipment."

The boys arrive home on Sunday night, dump all their equipment down, and their mother asks them, "Well, did you have a good time? Did you have the right stuff?"

"Oh, yeah, Mom, it was great. Dad said they were just the right skis and boots."

One month later, Steve is on the phone with Amy.

"What the dickens are all these bills for the kids?" Steve asks. "I've never seen someone spend such a mound of money for two kids. Do they have to have all this stuff?"

"But it's just what you wanted them to have. You said so yourself."

"Yes, but not if it was going to cost this much."

"What do you think that stuff costs? Have you ever gone shopping with the kids?"

"It's got nothing to do with going shopping. You're out of control with the spending. I've never seen anyone with so little sense about how to spend a dollar."

Just as he was saying confusing and contradictory things as he was beginning to separate from you in Act I, Scene 4, "Pre-Separation Separating," he has continued that contradictory behavior. The opposing statements cover all aspects of your life.

You're a good mother. You're a terrible mother.

You're a spendthrift. You don't know how to take some money and make yourself look good.

You're opinionated. You're totally devoid of conviction.

You're a wonderful homemaker. The house is always a mess.

You don't have any friends. You're never home; all you do is go out with your friends.

You're a very giving person. Your heart is made of ice.

You're the greatest marketing director ZeeCorp could ever have. You don't know how to be successful in a job.

Your own mother doesn't like you. Your mother wants you over all the time.

People love to be with you. You don't know how to get along in a social setting.

Sometimes he says it to your face; sometimes he says it out of your earshot and you hear it secondhand. You feel confused, baffled, and hurt. How can he be saying these totally contradictory things about you? No one can be both a good mother *and* a terrible mother. No one can be both opinionated *and* totally without conviction. "I thought I was a good mother." You think back over all the years, from the time they were babies, about how hard you worked to be the best mother you could be. Then you start to think, "But if he says I was a terrible mother maybe I was a terrible mother. Yes, Timmy is having trouble with math in school and Josie's room is always a mess and I said I wouldn't lead the fundraising for the drama program this year and when he would come home from work sometimes Josie was on the phone with her friends and Timmy was out playing basketball when he should have been doing his homework. Maybe I was a terrible mother."

Seventeen-year-old Matthew and fifteen-year-old Mikey are at their father's house for the weekend, as they are every other week. As they sit around the dinner table about to dive into some ice cream and cookies, Matthew and Mikey's new stepmother says, "Your father tells me your mother was not a good mother." Matthew is very surprised to hear this comment and rushes immediately to defend his mother. "She is too a good mother. What do you mean by that?"

"I mean your father said she really didn't take care of you the way a mother should."

"Mom sure did take care of us. She's the only mother I know who is at every one of our games. And every night if we need help with our homework, she'll sit with us as long as we need her."

"Look, wouldn't your father have better judgment about what kind of mother she was? He has the perspective of a wise adult. He knows what's been going on since you were babies."

Matthew and Mikey say nothing because they've always been told not to argue with their elders, but inside they are confused and don't know what to think. Haven't they heard their father saying to their grandma and also to several of their friends' mothers that their mom brought them up very well? Hasn't their mom always been there for them as long as they can remember? When Matthew and Mikey come home to their mother on Sunday night they can't help telling her what their stepmother said. They can see she's wounded by the words as soon as they've said them but she says only, "Thank you for telling me, boys."

You're hearing totally contradictory reviews of your life performance. You're hurt and confused. "Is it just me," you may wonder, "or does every woman feel this way?" Every woman feels this way.

TIP: LET NEITHER PRAISE NOR CRITICISM TURN YOUR PRETTY HEAD.

He has other audiences in mind and he wants favorable reviews from all of them. But just reading from the Script, willy-nilly, wherever he is, without considering the audience will not elicit favorable reviews. Like millions of men before him, he's going into improv and taking his cues from the audience. If they like his lines, they'll nod, laugh, and smile and he'll give them more of the same. If a line elicits a frown, criticism, or disapproval, he'll improvise and morph to match his surroundings.

The constant interplay of this improv, the audience reaction, and his subtle response to elicit an even better reaction creates an ever-improving performance sure to elicit rousing applause from every audience member, no matter which stage set he is performing on.

In a typical performance in this act of the play, he walks into the theater and sees that he will be performing on two stage sets.

On stage set A, the story lines are going back and forth with those who knew his first wife. He has learned from other men that he must go into improv and he has absorbed, from listening to other men, which story lines are likely to get this audience nodding in approval. All of them are variations on this essential theme: She's a good person, I'm a good person, no one did anything wrong, and no one is hurt. It just wasn't meant to be.

The audience breaks into applause. He truly is a great improv actor. He takes his bow on stage set A. As the applause dies down, those who know his first wife leave the theater with these variations on the "good person" story to tell and retell:

"She's a wonderful homemaker but they were just too much alike."

"She's a very good person but they were just too different."

"She's great with the kids, but a full life means more than that."

"They're both very good people but things happen."

"A fine couple but you know they just didn't have shared interests."

"Look, they're being civil with each other so nobody's hurt."

On stage set B he also goes into improv and co-creates a story that will have this audience, people in his new circle, nodding in approval. They leave the theater with variations on the "She was crazy" theme to tell and retell:

"No man could stay with a bitch like that."

"After all he's been through, he deserves his happiness."

"She spent all his money. He was going to end up in the poorhouse. He had to leave."

"She was crazy, really crazy. For his own sanity he had to leave."

"She wasn't a good mother. The kids were growing up to be spoiled brats."

"Did you hear how she dressed? He couldn't leave the house with her."

He gets favorable reviews, even some raves if he's particularly talented, because he has followed the successful Method acting of other men in co-creating the improv script with their audiences.

You will feel less hurt and confused if you know that he's just following the Script. For unfaithful men, even improv is part of the Script.

TIP: WRITE YOUR OWN REVIEWS

Don't let the praise and criticism you're hearing change your own review of your life performance. We guess it will read: "A natural. Did a really good job of playing multiple roles. Amazing instincts. Will only get better as time goes on."

FINALE

The chorus is ready to come on stage, but the composition of the chorus is different. The director found that they were just not singing together in harmony. Most of the women could not synchronize their voices with those of the seemingly happily divorced men. The divorced men who questioned their decision in retrospect could not keep this tone of dissonance out of their performance. The couples in the mixed chorus found the only lines they were comfortable with were platitudes.

So the director has divided them into three ensembles: an all-male group singing backup, an all-male anti-modern dissonant group, and a mixed choir singing harmony. He has even assigned them different dressing rooms so that they don't disturb each other.

Coming onto the risers now is the all-male backup ensemble. They enter with a confident gait, each one jostling for position to make sure the audience gets to see how young, vibrant, and successful he looks. Their diverse and attention-getting attire is unusual for a chorus: resort clothes, expensive Italian suits, studied business casual, each man dressed to project an image twenty years younger than he really is. Some appear not to have had a chance to change at all before coming on stage—one tenor is dressed in a deep-sea-diving suit, another comes on in high-performance mountain climbing attire along with all his rappelling equipment, another is dressed like a race car driver and is carrying his crash helmet. They start singing:

> *"She's young and beautiful. How happy I am."*
> *"I've never felt so young in my life."*
> *"I feel alive."*
> *"I'm a hero, a knight, a courageous chap."*
> *"We're still friends."*
> *"The kids are doing great."*

The male dissonant ensemble waits to come on until the backup chorus has completely exited the stage. These men walk in slowly. They are subdued and conservatively dressed. Some have children's toys hanging from their belt loops, some have bills stuffed in their breast pockets, and some get on the risers and immediately start to make phone calls—to the first wife, to the second wife, to the children, to their mothers.

The orchestra pit is again empty. Then one lone musician enters—a trumpet player. He picks up his horn and starts with . . . no, it can't be . . . what's the matter . . . he starts with . . . Taps? Some audience members assume the play is over and start to leave, but then they hear the chorus start to sing and sit down again. The dissonants sing prayerfully with a strain of longing in every note:

> *"What was I thinking?"*
> *"Now I see what I had."*
> *"I pray every day my children will say, 'Dad, it's okay, we forgive*
> *   you.' "*
> *"I miss my wife."*
> *"I miss my kids."*
> *"I'm telling you all, don't do it."*

The audience seems restless and uncomfortable. Where is the excitement, the feeling of paradise on earth, the look into a dreamy life? This scene is plain and everyday, too close to reality to have any escape value as a good play should. The costumes are somber, the trumpet player is laying on a continuously wailing note, and the lyrics sound like Sunday morning in church. No, some members of the audience think, I don't want to hear this.

Then the director brings his baton down. Silence descends. And the male dissonants leave the stage. The director wipes his brow. He has rehearsed them and rehearsed them, but this group just didn't carry the sense of their character through from beginning to end. Were they on a false note at the beginning or at the end? The director sees the mixed chorus waiting to come on and has no time to ponder this anymore.

A mixed chorus, smaller and different from the original one, now comes on. This group is composed of couples who sing only the lyrics of polite society and allow no note of counterpoint to intrude. They have arranged themselves into couples and look very decorous and proper. They stand tall, look straight ahead, and pass no judgment. They start to sing:

> *"We're friends with both of them."*
> *"Everyone seems to be doing fine."*
> *"We have no idea how they're doing. We don't ask questions."*
> *"What's done is done. You can't look back."*
> *"The future of the future is the future. And that's that."*
> *"Letting us know how they really feel won't help. We're glad they have the sense to keep it to themselves."*
> *"All's well that ends well."*

Jerry walks into the Bullseye Sports Bar just off the main drag in Rochester and joins a group of his friends with whom he gets together every Monday night. As they down the first of their beers, their attention is on the football game on the big screen. Then, as the game becomes one-sided, they start on some loud, back-slapping stories. In the middle of this Dean says to Jerry, "How's the old lady? How's things going on the home front?"

Jerry replies, "I'm thinking of splitting. I'm thinking of moving out. I'm just not happy."

Some of the other guys in the group hear this exchange. It's nothing new. Six of them have already split with their first wives and all six have remarried. The other six in the group of fast friends have mentioned thinking about it and have plenty of gripes about their wives but have never done anything beyond that. From stories Jerry has heard many men tell, when he says "I'm thinking of splitting" he is expecting to hear "Dump the bitch." So he is somewhat surprised when several of the six who were divorced and remarried say, "If you can possibly avoid it, don't do it."

It's 9:00 A.M. in Courtroom A in Family Court in Phoenix. Present in the courtroom are Patty and Mike, their lawyers and legal assistants. Soon the court will be called to order and the judge will start to decide on division of the couple's property and on support for Patty and the children.

Mike feels sure that everything will come out just as he has been planning. His lawyers have told him that he can expect to pay very modest support because the judge will agree that Patty and the children don't need much. Mike also anticipates no problems in keeping all the property he wants and in retaining the lion's share of the financial assets. He is the one who has earned the money, he has told his lawyers, and he is the one with far more substantial needs now.

The judge announces that she has a list of all the personal property the couple owns and that the process for dividing it will be that Mike and Patty will choose alternately from the list. A toss of the coin determines Mike will choose first. Then it is Patty's turn.

It goes back and forth. Soon it becomes apparent that it's not going the way Mike wants, not going the way he had mentally imag-
ined it. He's not getting some of the personal property he was
sure would be his. He is getting angrier and angrier, and finally
says out loud, "This is not the way I planned it." Everyone in the
courtroom bursts out laughing, including the judge.

All along he has been thinking, fantasizing, and imagining. Starting in Act I, Scene 7 ("This Could Work"), this mental rehearsal
has included the scenes being enacted in his mind of how his wife,
mistress, children, friends, lawyer, the judge, and the court will
play out their parts. He draws upon the success stories of other
men and their tales of how the people in their circle performed
their roles. If he hears a story of a difficult and unsuccessful outcome, our man ignores it because he feels "I'm different" (see Act
II, Scene 13). In fact, he very emphatically tells his friends how
wonderful things are with his new wife.

It's mid-afternoon at Porto Industries and it seems like everyone
in the IT department has come to the coffee room for an energy
boost. As they join a large group at the table, Zach says to Bert,
"Haven't seen you in a while. Where've you been?"

Bert replies, "Went on my honeymoon with Clarissa. You know
Bonnie and I divorced. Clarissa makes me so happy."

"How old is she?" Zach asks.

"Twenty-five," Bert answers.

"Jeeez," Chet lets out.

"You know, Bridget and I are living together since I left Joan," Sam
chimes in, "and I've never felt so young in my life."

"Yeah, you look great, Sam," Lou says.

"I'm thinking about starting afresh," Chet says. "Natalie wouldn't care. She doesn't really like me anyway."

"Go for it, guy," Steve says. "Rickie's done wonders for me."

But it almost never turns out the way he thinks it will. He may realize that it hasn't turned out the way he planned it, but he would never admit it. He would look foolish if he let on that he had given up so much and gotten nothing out of it. But he may think it to himself. Other men won't make negative comments about divorce around him because they know they would be raining on his wonderful parade. They will only start to make negative comments if he "gives permission" by starting to make negative comments himself, such as "Sometimes I have doubts about what I did." That's when you cue the male dissonant chorus.

Many things may not work out "the way he planned it," even sex with his new wife. You can see the progression as you watch the men's purchases in the La Femme Lingerie Shop.

Look at this married man coming in with his mistress. He is relishing buying her the whole set—low-cut French bra, tiny thong, lacy garter belt, and the sheerest lace top stockings. She talks about wanting to get married because she adores him. He comes back several times over the next year, always buying the sexiest bras, bikinis, garters, the whole shebang.

Then the couple's dreams come true. He's divorced and they're married. He comes into La Femme and buys her the sexiest set in the whole store. At home he gives it to her and she loves it.

The next time he comes into La Femme he tells Cherisse, the vendeuse, that he was told not to buy the bra anymore because she has to come in to try it on. Of course, she never had to try it on before.

Then he comes in late one afternoon some months later and says he wants to buy a sexy set but, as he said before, not the bra. Also Carrie, now his wife of nine months, told him not to buy the thong because it's too uncomfortable, just the garter belt and stockings.

Things are going well for the newly married couple but the next time Cherisse welcomes him to La Femme he says he was told only to buy some nice cotton underpants. That will do the job.

Our man may also find that he is socializing with a different group of people than he had planned. He finds he feels more comfortable around divorced people and they around him. Married couples he used to know may stay away because they find divorce threatening. Some old friends who feel close to his first wife may express their disapproval and discomfort by distancing themselves from him.

When he says, "This is not the way I planned it," you will see that your situations have been reversed. At the beginning of Act II, when he shocked you by dropping the Bomb, you were taken by surprise and were at a disadvantage because he knew the Script— his plan for what he was going to do and say from beginning to end. You most likely weren't prepared for this explosion and didn't have a plan.

Now you have learned from listening to your advisers—your lawyer, your counselor, a trusted relative, a CPA; from listening to other women; and from this very book—that you should start to plan as soon as possible. You have also gotten some good ideas about what that plan should include. So when you come to the Finale, you have a plan and know what to expect. He, on the other hand, has been living in a fantastical, semi-delusional state and doesn't know what to expect. That is why the sad, amazing, and absurd last line of the Script is, "This Is Not the Way I Planned It."

A Word to the Guys

Yes, we said at the end of Act I that the Word we gave you then was the first, last, and only word to the wise we were going to give you. This is just a reminder to read it again now that you've seen the fallout from Dropping the Bomb and everything that ensues from this in Act II.

Ask yourself if you really know the cost of what you're contemplating, or are you still living in the fantasy period, which never, ever lasts forever.